LEADERSHIP ENSEMBLE

LEADERSHIP ENSEMBLE

Lessons in Collaborative Management from the World's Only Conductorless Orchestra

Harvey Seifter, Executive Director
ORPHEUS CHAMBER ORCHESTRA
and Peter Economy

Foreword by J. Richard Hackman, Ph.D.

TIMES BOOKS
HENRY HOLT AND COMPANY • NEW YORK

Times Books
Henry Holt and Company, LLC
Publishers since 1866
115 West 18th Street
New York, New York 10011

Distributed in Canada by H. B. Fenn and Company Ltd.

Library of Congress Cataloging-in-Publication Data
Seifter, Harvey.
Leadership ensemble : lessons in collaborative management from the world's only conductorless orchestra / Harvey Seifter and Peter Economy.—1st ed.
p. cm.
Includes index.
ISBN 0-8050-6692-6
1. Teams in the workplace. 2. Orpheus Chamber Orchestra.
I. Economy, Peter. II. Title.
HD66 .S43 2001
658.4'036—dc21 2001037536

Henry Holt books are available for special promotions and premiums. For details contact: Director, Special Markets.

First Edition 2001

Designed by Kathryn Parise

Printed in the United States of America

10 9 8 7 6 5 4 3 2 1

To the members of Orpheus

ORPHEUS CHAMBER ORCHESTRA

2001

Violin

Ronnie Bauch
Martha Caplin
Nicolas Danielson
Guillermo Figueroa
Liang Ping How
Joanna Jenner
Todd Phillips
Eriko Sato
Naoko Tanaka
Eric Wyrick

Viola

Sarah Clarke
Maureen Gallagher
Nardo Poy

Cello

Eric Bartlett
Julia Lichten
Melissa Meell
Jonathan Spitz

Bass

Donald Palma

Flute

Susan Palma-Nidel

Oboe

Matthew Dine
Stephen Taylor

Clarinet

Charles Neidich
David Singer

Bassoon

Dennis Godburn
Frank Morelli

Horn

David Jolley
William Purvis

CONTENTS

FOREWORD

Less Is More

The Orpheus Chamber Orchestra often is described as a "leaderless" orchestra. It is true that one of the first things one notices about Orpheus is that there is no conductor signaling with baton and eyes and body how the music should be played. Yet Orpheus is anything but a leaderless orchestra. It has, in fact, *more* leadership than virtually any other organization I have seen in over a decade of research on group behavior and performance. Precisely because there is no conductor, each player must help decide about musical interpretations. Each one must take part of the responsibility for ensuring that musical entrances are together, that themes are passed smoothly from section to section, and that the composer's vision for a piece is realized beautifully and musically.

To attend an Orpheus concert or to listen to one of the orchestra's recordings is to experience a seamless musical performance. To watch an Orpheus rehearsal or recording session, on the other hand, is to see seams being stitched together, to watch democracy in action. My colleague Erin Lehman and I came away from our research at Orpheus with our belief in the power of democracy reaffirmed. But we also were reminded how challenging democracy can be. Orpheus musicians have to work nearly as hard in developing and exercising their leadership skills as they do in refining their talents as instrumentalists.

In midpassage at an Orpheus rehearsal one of the players rises unbidden from her seat, walks out into the concert hall where the rehearsal is being held, and listens intently for a few minutes. When she returns, her colleagues stop playing and look at her expectantly. She describes what she heard and makes a suggestion for improving the balance among the orchestra's sections. "Does anyone disagree?" she asks. No one does, and the violinist members had chosen as their concertmaster for that particular piece suggests that they try the passage again, this time with the violas a bit more prominent.

The piece being prepared involves a difficult transition from a solo passage played by a cellist to the woodwinds—just the kind of situation for which a cue from a conductor would be convenient, to say the least. The musicians talk it over and figure it out: the clarinetist has a clear view of the solo cellist, and will take his cue from her; the rest of the woodwinds will follow him.

The rehearsal stops. Should the passage just played have a light and lively spirit, or should it be more sedate? Opposing views about the composer's intentions are voiced. The orchestra tries the passage both ways but the disagreement persists. The concertmaster, who has been silent during the discussion and experimentation, eventually intervenes. "Let's take the lighter route," he says. The rehearsal continues without further comment.

Music is being made in these rehearsals, and all orchestra members have both a say in making it and a responsibility for how it turns out. The contrast with standard practice in conventional symphony orchestras could not be more striking. There, musicians do what they are told by the conductor and never, ever, offer up during rehearsal their own thoughts and ideas about musical interpretations. As a consequence, symphony orchestras leave a great deal of musical talent on the rehearsal stage. Members of the Orpheus Chamber Orchestra, by contrast, scoop up and use every scrap of talent they can find. (The contrast between Orpheus and professional symphony orchestras in leader roles and behaviors is illustrated in the video teaching case,

The Orpheus Chamber Orchestra, available from the Kennedy School of Government at Harvard University.)

It takes time to make music the Orpheus way—often thrice the time to prepare a piece as it would take if a conductor were calling the tune. Beyond that are orchestra meetings to attend and, for players who have been elected to leadership roles, decisions to make about repertoire, tours, guest soloists, and who will serve as concertmaster for what pieces on future programs.

Is it worth it? The Orpheus musicians would not have it any other way. And the acclaim that showers on the orchestra from audiences and critics affirms the musicians' conviction that this is a splendid way to make music. But it is hard, this business of making music democratically. It is hard because real democracy is not a simple one-person, one-vote decision-making process in which everyone's views count the same and consensus is easily achieved.

Orpheus musicians recognize that there are differences among players—in their experiences, in their musical perspectives, and in their special talents. At Orpheus, your say in a musical decision is not based on your age, or your gender, or your position, or how loudly you talk (well, at least not usually). At Orpheus, your say is determined by what you have to offer to the music. Contrary to what one might surmise from viewing a typical symphony orchestra concert, great music does *not* flow from the conductor's baton. It flows instead from the hearts and minds and musical souls of the players who are bringing the composer's vision to the audience. At Orpheus, there are twenty-seven hearts and minds and souls, every one of them a leader.

Are there lessons for the leaders of other organizations in how Orpheus musicians make their music? Yes, without question. The present book lays those lessons out in engaging and informative detail. As also will be seen in these pages, however, applying the principles of democracy to the daily work of purposive organizations is far from a walk in the park, even in the United States where the democratic ideal is vigorously espoused. Indeed, Orpheus itself has found it challenging to transfer the lessons that players have learned so well in the rehearsal hall to the orchestra's administrative offices, but, as this book documents, Orpheus members are committed to bringing what they have learned about shared leadership in music-making to the equally consequential task of running a music-making or other organization.

In reflecting on the experiences of this remarkable organization, its successes and the hurdles it has had to overcome, readers can learn a great deal about how more fully to engage the full complement of ideas, talents, and energy of people in their own enterprises. Moreover, readers can learn how to do that in a way that not only fosters the achievement of collective purposes but also contributes both to their organizations' ensemble qualities and to the lifelong learning and growth of individual members.

A decade ago, management guru Peter Drucker published an article in the *Harvard Business Review* in which he speculated about the implications of the information age for organizational structure and leadership ("The Coming of the New Organization," January-February 1988). Drucker suggested that large business organizations in the information age may well look less like traditional manufacturing companies and more like hospitals, universities, and symphony orchestras. In a large symphony orchestra, he pointed out, there is but a single conductor-CEO. Every one of the musicians, each a high-grade specialist, plays directly to that person without any middle-management intermediaries to make sure things go right. It is the job of the conductor, Drucker proposes, and increasingly will become the job of the CEO, to directly and insistently focus each player's skill and knowledge on the ensemble's joint performance.

The experience of the Orpheus Chamber Orchestra raises a strikingly different possibility. Rather than relying on a charismatic, visionary leader who both calls the shots and engages members' motivation, might it be possible for all members to share responsibility for leadership, and for their differences and disagreements to be sources of creativity rather than something that should be suppressed in the interest of uniformity and social harmony? This book offers an engaging and provocative view of what the latter option might look like—and suggests what it may take to get there from here.

J. Richard Hackman

INTRODUCTION

Carnegie Hall

It's Wednesday evening at Carnegie Hall. The air is charged with the excitement generated when people know that they are about to experience an event that will stimulate their senses and challenge their minds. It's the middle of the week, but the lobby is surprisingly crowded—people milling about, the atmosphere electric. In the bar area—its walls lined with autographed photos of many of the most famous and accomplished of Carnegie Hall's performers—people grab a quick glass of wine or cup of coffee and absorb a few moments of calm in anticipation of the coming musical storm.

Warm applause greets the members of Orpheus Chamber Orchestra as they take the stage. The musicians are the picture of confidence. Seasoned professionals, many of them record for the television and motion picture industry, play in other musical groups, and teach their chosen instruments at America's leading music schools, including Juilliard, the New England Conservatory, and the Manhattan School of Music. Carnegie Hall, one of the world's most prestigious performance venues, is Orpheus's home base; Orpheus and Carnegie Hall are linked in a formal partnership, a distinction we share with only one other orchestra.

But despite the group's home-team confidence, live performances—and audience response to them—are inherently unpredictable. Orpheus is venturing into uncharted territory with tonight's exploration of jazz-influenced classical music, and everyone in Carnegie Hall knows it.

In fact, creative tension, fueled by the presence of a new guest artist, famed jazz saxophonist Branford Marsalis, had been building within Orpheus ever since the orchestra gave the program its first tryout at a "run-out" concert in Purchase, New York, a few nights earlier. Although each individual piece sounded right, something about the mix and balance of the evening—the selection of music—was wrong. Orpheus faced two options: make the best of the existing program or make the more difficult, and potentially dangerous, choice of changing the program's content at the last minute.

We decided to fix the problem. By the second run-out concert in Easton, Pennsylvania, two nights later, Orpheus had won agreement from Marsalis and Sony Classical (which was recording the program the day after the Carnegie Hall concert and had strong opinions about the music it wanted us to perform) to make significant changes to the program. Orpheus substituted Debussy transcriptions for music by three other composers, and reordered the entire evening's musical flow. To accomplish this, new orchestrations had to be created overnight by an Orpheus member. Each musician in the orchestra learned the new music and the group worked together to reach immediate interpretive decisions about the music's sound.

Although this might seem to be a simple substitution to someone outside the music world, these changes are equivalent in magnitude to an executive team throwing out a substantial portion of their operating group's strategic plan and completely revising it just days before presentation to the company's board. In most other major musical organizations, making such changes to an established and rehearsed musical program just days before a Carnegie Hall concert would not even be considered, no matter how compelling the case to do so. But Orpheus is no ordinary orchestra.

When the musicians take their places on the stage, they concentrate on their final adjustments: checking their tuning, making sure the evening's music is arranged correctly (and in the right order) on their stands, and running through the opening notes one last time in their heads. As the members of Orpheus settle into their seats, it quickly becomes obvious to the audience that there's something different about this orchestra.

There's no conductor.

Orpheus Chamber Orchestra was founded in 1972 by cellist Julian Fifer and a small group of other musicians, including current members Joanna Jenner, David Jolley, and Don Palma, who aspired to create a new kind of orchestra, one that would liberate the creative energies of each musician and give every individual the power to direct great music.

Orpheus was designed to rely on the skills, abilities, and passionate commitment of its members rather than on the monolithic leadership of a conductor. The decision to give power to the musicians—a radical innovation in the orchestra world—required a structural model that was fundamentally different from the rigid command-and-control hierarchy universally employed by traditional orchestras. The original members of Orpheus found their inspiration in chamber music, a world grounded in democratic values, where small ensembles, generally fewer than ten musicians, function as self-managing teams, and where power, responsibility, leadership, and motivation rest entirely in the hands of the people doing the work.

Julian Fifer, who left the group in 1998, recalled the genesis of his idea for an orchestra with no conductor in an interview for *Fast Company* magazine. According to Fifer, "I loved chamber music's clarity of sound and flexibility of temperament. I wanted to bring that camaraderie and spirit into a larger setting. And in order for everyone to be able to communicate more effectively, it seemed necessary to do without a conductor." While there was no way that Fifer and friends could have foreseen exactly where this idea would take us, it was clear that they had chanced upon something special. According to Fifer, "We had no particular method for presenting interpretations and ideas on a piece, but our spirits were high, and we had a great deal of enthusiasm. It was as if we were calling out to anyone who would listen, 'Look Ma, no hands!' "[1]

Orpheus Chamber Orchestra is unique. Widely regarded as one of the world's great orchestras, we are the only major orchestra in the world to consistently rehearse, perform, and record without a conductor. For nearly thirty years, Orpheus has flourished as a self-governing organization; our members rotate their seating positions to give each player the opportunity to lead a section. Together they make the artistic decisions that are ordinarily the work of a conductor, and they actively participate in choosing the repertoire and creating the group's musical programs. This makes Orpheus a living, breathing laboratory for a new style of shared leadership based upon creative and engaged individuals, an agile and flexible organization, and the highest level of performance.

Although we have no conductor, we are most definitely not an organization without leadership. In fact, Orpheus has *many* leaders, and different individuals rise to leadership roles based on the orchestra's needs and the demands of each piece of music. Orpheus's beautiful and internationally renowned performances directly result from a management process that draws upon the most creative and productive capabilities of all the group's members. In that process are lessons for any company searching for new ways to bring out the excellence in its employees and in the products and services they deliver.

The challenge in today's technology-driven, speed-of-light business environment is constant and pervasive. With the tools contained herein, the reader will be able to translate the lessons that we have refined over the course of three decades and apply them to his or her own organization with predictable, immediate, and positive results.

1

Overture: The Rules Have Changed (Again)

More than a decade ago, management guru and visionary Peter Drucker predicted a time when the traditional, hierarchical management model would fall away, replaced by much more responsive, "flat" organizations. According to Drucker, "the typical large business twenty years hence will have fewer than half the levels of management of its counterpart today, and no more than a third of the managers. In its structure, and in its management problems and concerns, it will bear little resemblance to the typical manufacturing company, circa 1950, that our textbooks still consider the norm. Instead, it is far more likely to resemble organizations that neither the practicing manager nor the management scholar pays much attention to today: the hospital, the university, the symphony orchestra."[1]

Dramatic changes that rocked the business world over the past ten years have proved Drucker remarkably prescient. In most cases, management ranks that were decimated during the severe recession that gripped the American economy during the late 1980s and early 1990s were never rebuilt during the economic and employment boom that followed. Instead, the information technology revolution changed the rules of business once again, creating new consumer expectations for service and innovation, and a new class of worker—the *knowledge* worker—to fulfill them.

As the rate of technological change has continued to accelerate, so has the speed of business. Few things are guaranteed in today's world except this: If an organization can't respond quickly enough to change and the marketplace opportunities that change brings, its competition will.

Today's most successful companies use change to their advantage, reacting immediately to new challenges as they emerge and even anticipating shifts in their market, product development, and resource needs. Not surprisingly, corporations are increasingly turning to new models of leadership and management to help them keep up with the accelerating pace of change. According to C. K. Prahalad, a University of Michigan business professor who advises companies such as Citicorp, Eastman Kodak, and Oracle, "Speed is becoming the most important criterion for growth and survival. That is taking decision-making and accountability to levels that are closest to the business."[2] In the information economy, employees give corporations their most important competitive advantage. Companies that are adaptable enough to learn to solicit and utilize the talents and skills of each employee—no matter where he or she resides on the organization chart—will flourish.

Regrettably, many organizations are unable to respond to rapid change in the marketplace because they find themselves stymied by old-fashioned hierarchical management structures. Companies that are caught up in rigid policies and procedures, and overlook the potential of their employees to function as a vast well of talent within their organizations, simply can't compete anymore. There isn't time for decisions to work their way through multiple layers of management review and approval before they can be implemented.

For many organizations, it is too late to ponder whether or not replacing the old structures with something new is the right course. Nearly every day, yet another corporation falls by the wayside—a casualty of failing to harness the skills, creativity, and leadership talent of *all* its employees. Much of the blame for these failures can be placed on the near-religious conviction with which many managers still ascribe to the century-old findings of business researcher and theoretician Frederick Taylor.

Hierarchy Rules

Frederick Taylor pioneered the science of modern management. In his 1911 book, *The Principles of Scientific Management,* Taylor demonstrated that by breaking down work processes into a series of simple steps, and then measuring and optimizing the performance of each one, corporations are able to extract tremendous efficiency improvements from factory workers. Taylor's scientific techniques were revolutionary, and the most successful organizations of his day were the ones that were quick to adopt his ideas and put them into practice.

One of Taylor's fundamental assumptions, however—an assumption that became a cornerstone of "good" management practice through the rest of the twentieth century—was that workers lacked the basic knowledge and ability to truly understand their jobs. Taylor considered workers to be unpredictable and unreliable by nature. As he proclaimed in *The Principles of Scientific Management,* "The science which underlies each act of each workman is so great and amounts to so much that the workman who is best suited to actually doing the work is incapable of fully understanding this science."[3] Since workers couldn't be trusted to understand enough about their work to do the right job, in the right way, at the right time, a new class of employees was needed to coordinate and direct their activities. Almost overnight, professional managers became omnipresent in business, taking on considerable power and exerting control over workers by determining and evaluating almost every action that they took.

In the 1950s, a new kind of manager appeared on the corporate landscape—the "Organization Man." In his classic book by that name, William Whyte described a world where managers increasingly identified themselves with the corporations for which they worked, submerging their own identities in the process. While virtues such as entrepreneurship, individualism, and self-reliance had previously been the norms of business, the Organization Man favored the predictability of bureaucracy and a new set of workplace values: conformity and security. In effect, ever larger and more complex organizations had applied Taylor's decoupling of individual workers from responsibility and authority to higher and higher levels within their managerial hierarchies. The equation in business became, in Whyte's words, "Be loyal to the company, and the company will be loyal to you."[4]

This all changed radically, however, when the American economy was gripped by recession in the early 1990s, and hundreds of thousands of managers and workers alike found themselves downsized out of their formerly secure jobs. In this new leaner and meaner business environment, workers realized that no amount of loyalty could guarantee a job and companies discovered technology-enabled ways to empower workers that created new opportunities to decentralize management without sacrificing efficiency. Suddenly, the assets of the Organization Man became liabilities, as corporations began to flatten their hierarchies and implement policies that allowed more flexibility for workers in a drive to transform into more flexible, nimble, and entrepreneurial organizations.

However, despite the recent proliferation of "enlightened" workplace practices such as empowerment, self-managing work teams, and the like, employees report that when it comes to important matters, precious little has changed since Taylor's time. A survey of self-managing work teams found that in the overwhelming majority of cases, management still makes the most important decisions for the teams, including setting employee salaries, determining raises, hiring, firing, selecting team leaders, and designating overall team goals. Team members, who were repeatedly told by their bosses that they were being empowered to be leaders, were left with relatively trivial decisions regarding team process and function, such as when and where the team would meet and who would be responsible for taking notes.[5]

Hierarchy still rules.

Hierarchy in Information-Based Organizations

As Peter Drucker noted, orchestras, like hospitals and universities, are "information-based organizations," composed largely of specialists who direct and discipline their own performance through organized feedback from colleagues, customers, and the organization's management.

Orchestras add one more element to the mix: a single manager who leads the organization in preparation (rehearsal) and execution (performance)—the conductor. A conductor's work, as portrayed by Elizabeth Green in *The Modern Conductor,* might also describe a successful CEO leading *any* organization: "To stand in front of an orchestra, band, or chorus and beat time does not make one a conductor. But to bring forth thrilling music from a group of singers or players, to inspire them (through one's own personal magnetism) to excel, to train them (through one's own musicianship) to become musicians themselves, personally to feel the power of music so deeply that the audience is lifted to new heights emotionally . . . yes, *this* can be called conducting."[6]

But the job of conducting encompasses much more than inspiration and education. Conductors are also specifically trained to micromanage. They select the music and the musicians who play it, and determine exactly how each piece will sound by making thousands of decisions about tempo, phrasing, volume, and balance—details that govern each musician's playing and ultimately determine the character of the musical performance. Conductors are expected to have strong opinions, backed by knowledge about the technical capabilities and challenges of each instrument of the orchestra. These opinions are rarely open for question or discussion.

Conductors stand at the very pinnacle of their orchestras' musical hierarchies, in roles that go far beyond those of most corporate CEOs or presidents. Instead of directly supervising the activities of a relatively small team of vice presidents or top managers as do most chief executives, conductors directly supervise the activities of each and every musician in the orchestra. They are expected to exact uniformity from large groups, down to the smallest details, and any failure to invoke that authority is likely to be perceived as weakness. When asked if the orchestra conductor is a good model for leadership in business, Ben Zander, founder and conductor of the Boston Philharmonic Orchestra, was unequivocal in his response. "It's the worst! The conductor is the last bastion of totalitarianism in the world—the one person whose authority never gets questioned. There's a saying: Every dictator aspires to be a conductor."[7]

Many conductors are resistant, if not downright hostile, to receiving input from the musicians who actually play the music. Such conductors literally rule their orchestras with an iron baton. The stories are legendary. Zander recounts one about the renowned maestro Arturo Toscanini: "It is said that once in the middle of a rehearsal, in a fit of anger, he fired a long-standing member of the double bass section, who now had to return home to tell his wife that he was out of a job. As the bass player packed up his instrument, he mentioned a few things that he had hitherto kept to himself, and, as he left the hall for the final time, shouted at Toscanini, 'You are a no-good son of a bitch!' So oblivious was Toscanini to the notion that a player would dare to challenge his authority, that he roared back: 'It is too late to apologize!' "[8]

With such attitudes, it's not surprising that orchestral musicians tend to keep their most original and creative impulses to themselves, rather than risk the fury of a conductor who neither wants nor expects input. The inevitable result is that the musicians are detached from their product, the music they create with their instruments. Says jazz guitarist Mark Worrell, "In a symphonic context, you find 'workers' with fabulous talents, formal training, and an abundance of theoretical knowledge, and yet strangely enough these musicians are forced to separate their capacity for conceptualization from the moment of execution. This is an incredibly authoritarian and antidemocratic model of musical production. It would not be an exaggeration to state that the symphony itself is a mass celebration of authoritarianism—perhaps even charismatic dictatorship."[9]

This kind of environment makes the traditional symphony orchestra a prime example of the tension that exists between traditional hierarchy's command-and-control structures and the knowledge worker's inherent bias toward self-management. Since it is the knowledge workers who provide the intellectual and creative capital that drive all information-based organizations, alternative management models that succeed in transforming the orchestra can have potentially wide-ranging applicability.

THE ORPHEUS PROCESS: NO CONDUCTOR, MANY LEADERS

Orpheus Chamber Orchestra has developed just such an alternative model. Our approach to orchestral leadership—eliminating the role of the conductor and dividing those responsibilities among the twenty-seven members of the orchestra—is radically different from that employed by any other orchestra in the world.

Orpheus has many leaders. Individual musicians constantly rotate formal leadership roles, while others spontaneously take on ad hoc leadership responsibilities in response to organizational needs and the specific demands of each piece of music. In fact, everyone in Orpheus is expected to become a leader at some time, ensuring that we sustain a unique multileadered organization that fully engages and flexibly deploys the creative abilities and energies of each member. Time and again in my years with Orpheus, I have seen this reservoir of leadership give the group an unparalleled range and depth of talent to draw upon in performance. This extraordinary organizational resource has fueled Orpheus's three-decade success story.

The Orpheus Process has been refined over the years to allow the group to consistently and efficiently transfer the communal creativity of a small, four-piece chamber music group into the much larger setting of an orchestra, which can sometimes swell to forty musicians or more. There are five key elements:

1. **Choosing Leaders.** For each piece of music performed by Orpheus, the musicians select a leadership team of five to ten players, called the core.

A committee of musicians, themselves elected by all the members of the orchestra, selects a concertmaster, the first-chair violinist who in chamber music ensembles is traditionally recognized as "first among equals" and in conducted orchestras has a role in some ways analogous to a shop foreman. In Orpheus, the concertmaster anchors the core, leads performances, and works closely with all the musicians to develop a unified vision for the music along the way. Other instrumental sections (cellos, oboes, etc.) then choose individuals to represent them on the leadership team.

2. **Developing Strategies.** The core meets to decide how the selected piece of music will be played, developing an overall interpretive approach to the music before it is taken to the full orchestra. These meetings take the form of rehearsals where many different approaches can be tried in a streamlined fashion.
3. **Developing the Product (the Music).** When the core is satisfied with its approach to the piece, it is taken to the full orchestra to be rehearsed and refined even further. Immediately after each piece is played in rehearsal, musicians from throughout the orchestra call out suggestions to improve the interpretation or to critique the playing of their fellow orchestra members. Sometimes smaller debates over style, tempo, balance, and other musical nuances ensue within the different sections of the orchestra. When disagreements arise, the members of the orchestra work to reach a consensus—hashing out the issues face-to-face, in real time. If they still can't reach an agreement after a reasonable period of debate, then a vote is taken and the issue is settled.
4. **Perfecting the Product (the Music).** Immediately before every concert, a small number of members are deputized to leave their seats onstage and go out into the hall, so they can suggest final adjustments and refinements based on the actual sound of the full orchestra.
5. **Delivering the Product (the Music).** The final step is performance, the ultimate result of the Orpheus Process. After each concert, the members

of the orchestra talk to one another about ideas for further refinements to the piece—ideas that may make their way into the next performance.

The focal point of the Orpheus Process is the musicians themselves. Every aspect of their performance begins and ends with the full orchestra. Cellist Eric Bartlett, who like many Orpheus members plays with other, more traditional groups as well, sees a significant difference between the music produced by Orpheus and that produced by other groups. Says Eric, "When there's an important concert, everybody goes into it doing their absolute best work, giving it their utmost concentration, playing off of each other, and making sparks fly. For the most part, in a conducted orchestra, you play a more passive role. Not only is less expected *of* you, but less is expected *from* you. You have to play extremely well, but you're not playing off of your colleagues—you're playing off of that one person in front of the orchestra holding the baton. Everybody plays well, they do a very good job, but the level of individual emotional involvement isn't there."

Orpheus's work is most fundamentally defined by the tremendous power and authority wielded by the musicians throughout the organization, rather than by the absence of a conductor. In the words of Michael Wiener, cofounder of Infinity Broadcasting and vice chairman of the Orpheus board of trustees, "Orpheus is unique because musicians call the shots—it's rare to have performers so involved in the process of running an orchestra. But the result is obvious: a better, more musical and emotionally engaged performance."

In traditional orchestras, the board of trustees, administrative management, and (of course) the conductor play the key roles in determining strategic direction, project selection, and resource allocation. In Orpheus, the musicians participate in all areas of organizational decision making and every day they work closely with me to develop ideas for new projects, repertoire, and artistic development. The structure of Orpheus reflects the power of musicians throughout the organization—members of the orchestra elect rotating representatives who serve in the management structure and on the board of trustees. We will explore these different roles in much greater detail in upcoming chapters.

The Orpheus Process and its underlying principles, such as passionate dedication to mission, shared and rotated leadership, clarity of roles, and more have served us well, producing four Grammy Awards and nearly thirty years of creative innovation and sustained musical excellence at the highest levels of international accomplishment. The Orpheus principles and process form the foundation of a collaborative management structure that has sustained our success in the business of music as well, including record production and sales, tours, new media contracts, and corporate sponsorships. As a group, Orpheus employees are extremely dedicated and entrepreneurial. Unafraid to take risks, they work hard to find new ways of achieving critical acclaim, artistic excellence, and full involvement.

But can the principles and process work outside of our musical laboratory—within, for example, a Fortune 500 firm, a technology start-up, or century-old not-for-profit organization? We believe they can, and our belief is shared by dozens of organizations that have asked us to provide live demonstrations of the Orpheus Process, including Novartis, the University of Chicago Business School, Kraft Foods, Hitotsubashi University's International Center for Strategic Management, Voluntary Hospitals of America, Morgan Stanley, and the Arthur W. Page Society. Says the *New York Times*, "Orpheus has more in common with some of America's largest companies than the casual observer might think. The group has become a living, and entertaining, microcosm of a management theory that has been transforming corporate America throughout the 1990s."[10]

The Eight Orpheus Principles

The Orpheus Process and the orchestra's success are founded on eight core principles. In the chapters that follow, we will examine how each of these principles allows us to consistently bring out the best in each member of our team. We'll also see how these very same principles play a critical role in the success of some of today's most dynamic companies, and how they can bring out the best in *your* organization.

The eight Orpheus principles are:

1. **Put power in the hands of the people doing the work.** We believe that an organization's creative potential can only be fully realized when its members are given the authority to make decisions that have impact. Power and decision-making authority are widely distributed and exercised throughout Orpheus, unleashing a great deal of energy onstage and behind the scenes.
2. **Encourage individual responsibility.** With authority comes responsibility. Each member of Orpheus takes personal responsibility for ensuring that our products are of the very highest quality. Instead of waiting for a supervisor to flag or fix problems, individuals take the initiative to resolve issues as expeditiously as possible.
3. **Create clarity of roles.** Unclear roles can lead to employee conflict, wasted effort, poor morale, and, ultimately, poor products. By clearly defining roles and functions throughout the organization, Orpheus minimizes confusion and ensures that each individual's energies are most effectively focused.
4. **Share and rotate leadership.** Orpheus encourages everyone to lead at some point, in some way—in fact, we insist on it. We believe that every employee has something of value to contribute, and that by sharing and rotating leadership, organizations can benefit from the unique skills and experience of each individual.
5. **Foster horizontal teamwork.** Orpheus depends on cross-organizational teams and teamwork built on wide-ranging personal expertise and individual responsibility. We have seen time and again how teams with individual and group authority reduce the time it takes to make informed decisions and ensure that everyone works together to achieve goals.

6. **Learn to listen, learn to talk.** The Orpheus Process requires open channels of communication to work at peak efficiency. Everyone in our organization is expected to listen actively and intently, and to speak directly and honestly. Without a constant flow of two-way communication, the process cannot succeed.
7. **Seek consensus (and build creative structures that favor consensus).** Our group cannot move forward unless its members agree to move together in the same direction at the same time. Seeking—and finding—consensus is a vital element in how Orpheus gets things done. Since we can't always reach consensus, we also have clear and effective mechanisms in place to resolve deadlock.
8. **Dedicate passionately to your mission.** Above all, Orpheus Chamber Orchestra is marked by our passionate dedication to our mission. That passion drives every musical and business decision that we make. Our organization's mission isn't imposed from above, but is determined—and constantly refined—by the members themselves.

We wrote this book to provide you with an insider's view of the Orpheus Process and the eight principles that make it work. Although each of the next eight chapters is organized around one of these principles, in some cases the principles inevitably overlap. For example, you will find references to teamwork in the chapter about putting power in the hands of the people doing the work (chapter 2) and a discussion about the importance of good communication in the chapter about sharing and rotating leadership (chapter 5). The Orpheus Process is a dynamic synthesis of these eight principles, and our objective is to shed light on how our management structure works, rather than to create rigid categories and rules.

In addition to taking a thorough look at how each of the eight principles works within Orpheus, we have selected a variety of businesses to illustrate how these same principles work in other organizations. These organizations—including J. P. Morgan Chase, Morgan Stanley, the Ritz-Carlton Hotel Company, W. L. Gore Associates, the San Diego Zoo, Russell Reynolds Associates, Intel, Sturman Industries, Stonyfield Farm, and many more—have all found great success by applying the principles that form the foundation of the Orpheus Process.

Finally, we end each chapter with a five-step "prescription" for how you might apply the relevant principle to your company, and a warning about potential problems and pitfalls you may encounter in doing so.

It's our sincere hope that this book will introduce you to some new ways of doing business, ways that will help you create a more effective organization, happier and more engaged employees, and satisfied clients and customers. We know that every corporation contains a tremendous wellspring of creativity and energy—its people. By following the eight principles in this book, you'll be able to unleash this creativity and energy—just as we have.

2

Put Power in the Hands of the People Doing the Work

Powerlessness corrupts.
Absolute powerlessness corrupts absolutely.

—ROSABETH MOSS KANTER,
PROFESSOR, HARVARD BUSINESS SCHOOL

In recent years, most managers have become very familiar with the mantra of empowerment. According to this mantra, employers who give every worker the responsibility for performing meaningful tasks and the authority to get jobs done are rewarded with an empowered workforce composed of contented and loyal employees, who in turn make their customers happy as well. However, while many companies have taken on the symbolic trappings of empowerment by trimming multiple levels of management and giving nonmanagerial workers new titles and job descriptions, how many have granted employees real, meaningful power?

The truth is that few employees—even among so-called empowered corporations—have any say in setting the goals and direction of the companies they work for. In most organizations, authority to decide what products and services to provide to customers, and how best to provide them, still remains closely held by management at levels far removed from either product creation or service delivery. A Gallup survey of twelve hundred U.S. workers demonstrates that the reality of worker empowerment is quite different than the story touted by today's "enlightened" businesses. While an impressive 66 percent of survey respondents reported that their managers asked them to *get involved* in decision making, only 14 percent felt that they had actually been given real authority.[1] Apparently, it's one thing to talk about empowerment, but it's another to give it.

The symphony orchestra is a particularly stark example of the virtually complete powerlessness still facing so many knowledge workers. A conductor communicates with the more than one hundred musicians "reporting" to him by standing on an elevated platform and waving a stick of wood at them. This communication is essentially one-way since individual musicians rarely—if ever—express an idea or opinion to the conductor. Orchestral musicians are constantly required to conform, and they are usually denied an individual sense of accomplishment. For example, in a traditional orchestra, an important element of the job of violinist number 26 is to make absolutely sure that his bow flies off the strings of his instrument at precisely the same nanosecond as violinists number 25 and number 27. If he does his job well, violinist 26's immediate feedback (and reward) is to be ignored by the conductor altogether. Creativity, engagement in the process, and employee satisfaction don't really enter into the equation.

Unfortunately, to many workers in a wide variety of industries, this scenario will sound all too familiar. At the very least, top-down tyranny in the workplace leads to poor morale, low retention rates, and significant opportunity costs for the entire organization. In extreme cases, the results can include poor products and inadequate services, leading to less than satisfactory customer experiences. Clearly, organizations that put power in the hands of the people doing the work enjoy a substantial competitive advantage over those who do not.

THE PRINCIPLE

Empowerment means many things to many companies. At Target department stores, it means giving cashiers the authority to ask customers if they know the price of an unmarked item and then, if it sounds reasonable, entering that price in the cash register without further approval from management. Customers save time while paying for their purchases, employees are happier because they know that management trusts their judgment, and managers are freed up to concentrate on more productive tasks. At aerospace giant Boeing, a "no messenger" rule puts an enormous amount of power in the hands of workers: members of employee teams are *required* to make their own decisions concerning matters within their purview. To reinforce this, team members are not permitted to take unresolved issues to supervisors for a decision.

When we talk about putting power in the hands of the people doing the work, we are specifically suggesting giving workers the ability to exercise some measure of authority over such areas as setting work schedules and environment, developing and executing budgets, hiring and firing employees, determining what products and services will be developed and sold, and participating in the development of mission, strategy, and goals. Companies that do so will garner:

- Increased employee engagement in their jobs
- Improved worker morale in response to increased management trust
- New ideas, fresh energy, and increased employee commitment to achieving the corporation's goals
- Decreased employee absenteeism and rates of turnover

As we in Orpheus and banking giant J. P. Morgan Chase have seen, the benefits of putting power in the hands of the people doing the work go far beyond simply building a happy workforce.

ORPHEUS: A DEMOCRACY AT WORK

Unlike most orchestras, Orpheus has a strong and deeply rooted democratic tradition. By careful design, our twenty-seven permanent musicians wield real power over the creative and artistic process, and they have a significant voice in the organization's overall direction. Our musicians decide for themselves who will lead them onstage, and who will represent them on the board and within the administrative management. In a *New York Times* interview, oboist Matthew Dine described Orpheus's working environment as a place where "anyone can say anything they want and generally they do. During the discussions the interpretation forms itself. That doesn't mean that we have control over everything. Spontaneous things happen onstage, and sometimes after a performance we're saying, 'How did we do that?' But we go out knowing we're ready."[2]

Empowering musicians was—and still is—a radical innovation in the orchestra world. After nearly thirty years of experience, we can summarize the extraordinary results as follows: empowerment gives us the ability to maximize the talents of highly skilled individuals throughout our organization, and it improves our performance across the full spectrum of our activities.

The Chamber Music Paradigm

The founders of Orpheus required a model that was fundamentally different from the rigid and hierarchical structures of traditional orchestras, which were populated with authoritarian conductors, star soloists, and anonymous instrumentalists. To find it, they had to look to classical music's other group performance scenario—chamber music—for clues.

Solo performers are, along with conductors, the stars of the field. They have virtually unrestricted power over their own performances, and they exert a substantial amount of control over other musicians' work as well. Not surprisingly, soloists frequently grow accustomed to dominating the final product, and come to believe that the role of every other musician onstage is to support their work. Orchestral musicians, on the other hand, are expected to follow direction as quickly, efficiently, and unobtrusively as possible. Technical proficiency and reliability are the most important factors in job performance.

The vast majority of musicians begin their careers as aspiring soloists, but only a small number possess the requisite mix of talent, charisma, endurance, and bravado needed to succeed. Although some musicians choose to play in orchestras because that experience most closely corresponds to their interests and temperaments, most orchestral musicians end up on this professional track either because teachers directed them to it, or because they were forced there by intense competition.

In many respects, the role of a soloist closely resembles that of a star salesperson, engineer, or software developer in the corporate world. Some amount of impetuousness, individuality, and originality is not only expected but encouraged in these business "soloists"—especially if the result is increased sales or product breakthroughs for the company. In business, the orchestral musician's role falls to the bulk of so-called rank-and-file workers. Regardless of how challenging their jobs may be, or how much creativity and originality may go into their performance, most workers are expected to simply do their jobs in compliance with company policies and procedures. While workers in some companies have a voice in setting goals and defining their jobs, most do not and often managers can overrule or "improve" employee-set goals.

Orpheus's founders discovered their inspiration in chamber music, a world grounded in democracy, where power along with responsibility, leadership, and motivation lie entirely in the hands of the people doing the work. Chamber musicians take personal responsibility for their performances while relying, to an astounding degree, on trust in the other musicians to determine the quality and character of the group's finished product.

In chamber ensembles, musicians bring their own ideas, energies, passions, and creativity to their music-making, working in close and fundamentally equal collaboration with other musicians and exercising self-evaluation to improve performance. Each participant individually negotiates the balance between independent thinking and teamwork. Many orchestral musicians and even instrumental soloists also belong to one or more chamber groups, not for financial benefit or professional advantage (indeed, they may not even perform chamber music for the public) but rather for their own pleasure.

Chamber musicians experience feelings of collegiality, shared purpose, and decision-making authority. These are powerful motivational forces that have broad applicability to the challenge of managing today's knowledge workers; clearly, chamber ensembles serve as a perfect analogue for business's self-managing teams.

Our unique approach brings this chamber music ideal to the experience of playing in an orchestra. In Orpheus, the orchestra stars, and every member gets the opportunity to solo. For a performance to reach its full potential, everyone has to be fully engaged.

The Fundamentals

During Orpheus's early years, our founding members identified a set of fundamental rules to guide them as they created a new orchestral structure. According to Norma Hurlburt, former executive vice president and general manager of Orpheus, these guidelines served either to give power to the musicians or help exercise power effectively:

- Management does not impose its vision on the musicians.
- Disputes are settled by vote of all members.
- Membership in the orchestra is decided by orchestra members.
- Interaction in rehearsal is essential, with civility and trust valued as operating norms.[3]

With these guidelines, Orpheus built a culture for employee authority, a necessary groundwork for finding a new way of making music and doing business. Thirty years later, they still apply.

Diffusing the Conductor's Authority

The absence of a conductor at the front of the orchestra does not mean that we have jettisoned authority. In fact, the reality is quite the opposite. Says violinist Ronnie Bauch, "No orchestra exists without direction, and the absence of a conductor as central authority figure doesn't mean that power doesn't exist. Power *needs* to exist. The unique thing about Orpheus is that power is divided up. At the basis of what we do, diversity is our strength. Empowering individual musicians allows Orpheus to draw on the leadership potential of everyone in the organization."

In Orpheus, we continuously disperse the conductor's traditional power and authority among everyone in the orchestra, and all members own an equal share. Members play active roles in key decision-making processes, including selecting music, determining the orchestra's interpretation, and finding the best way to contribute their specialized skills to the group as a whole. Working together on a self-managed basis, the musicians decide who will be invited to join our group (and, perhaps, who will be invited to leave), designate leaders for each piece, plan and implement rehearsal processes, and make the hundreds of interpretive decisions that shape the final performance. "Of course," says Bauch, "the trick is to coordinate all this diverse opinion and input."

Granting members the conductor's authority enhances our musical product by allowing us to draw on the expertise and leadership ability of many highly skilled musicians. It also creates an environment where employees know their contributions are welcome and valued. According to Orpheus bassoonist Frank Morelli, "What's special about Orpheus is the fact that, like a chamber ensemble, we work out our own interpretation, and we've been able to have an impact on artistic decisions such as personnel and repertoire. In Orpheus, one doesn't feel like a cog in a wheel. We are enfranchised, what we do is highly valued and it has the potential of having an impact upon the result. That puts us in a different frame of mind as far as how we can—and are expected to—contribute to the situation."

The average tenure in our orchestra is eighteen years and growing. While our members do occasionally choose to leave the group, most consider their participation in Orpheus to be the most exciting and fulfilling aspect of their professional lives, and will do whatever it takes to protect their tenure. High on the list of reasons for this dedication is empowerment.

For double-bass player Don Palma, a founding member, a brief foray into the world of conducted orchestras proved to be an experience that he didn't soon wish to repeat. Says Palma, "I took one year off from Orpheus at the very beginning and went to the Los Angeles Philharmonic. I just hated it. I didn't like to be told what to do all the time, being treated like my only value was just to sit there and be a good soldier. I felt powerless to affect things, particularly when they were not going well. I felt frustrated, and there was nothing I could seem to do to help make things better." As a member of Orpheus, however, life is quite different. In Palma's words, "Orpheus keeps me involved. I have some measure of participation in the direction the music is going to take. I think that's why a lot of us have stayed involved for so long."

The Power of Decentralization

In the past, businesses could maintain competitive advantage by concentrating power and decision making at the very top of the organization. Those days are now behind us. According to business researchers Eli Cohen and Noel Tichy, "In slower, more predictable times, command-and-control hierarchies weren't such a bad idea. They provided a simple system for consistent decision making: All questions were passed up the ladder to the same small group of people, and their decisions were handed back down. But in the current wired-together global marketplace, pleasing customers and making a profit are functions of quick thinking and agile action. In the time it takes for a question to be passed up the ladder and a decision handed back down, a customer may have gone elsewhere, or the opportunity may be lost."[4]

Gonzalo de Las Heras, executive vice president of international banking giant Banco Santander Centro Hispano (BSCH) and chairman of the Orpheus board of trustees, believes that the power of decentralized decision making is a key advantage of our organization, one that can help *any* business stay ahead of the competition. According to Las Heras, "What I've found in business is that some employees—particularly young people—don't want to decide on their own, because they're afraid. Of course, if you just sit passively, receive orders, and carry them out, you won't produce change or innovation, regardless of how much talent you bring to your endeavors. We have to encourage employees to create, to speak up and to find new and better ways of doing things, by making them partners. People fight much harder for the decision that they've made themselves. They feel that they own it. They work harder on making it a success because it's their own decision." As the speed of business continues to accelerate, the ability to foster innovation in a changing environment is a key ingredient in successful organizations.

The Product of Empowerment

Like the members of a string quartet, the twenty-seven members of Orpheus are directly responsible for many of our organization's most fundamental and important product decisions. It's the musicians who figure out how to adapt Friday night's successful performance in a four-hundred-seat hall in Easton, Pennsylvania, to the special needs of Carnegie Hall with its twenty-eight hundred seats, and implement the changes in an hour or two on Saturday morning.

To do so, we have developed formal structures to ensure that musicians have real power throughout the organization and participate in all important decisions.

Orpheus is a nonprofit corporation and, by law, the board of trustees is the ultimate repository of authority within our organization. Our board acts in much the same capacity as the board of directors in a for-profit corporation (with the important difference that our board is responsible to the "public trust" rather than to shareholders), working to ensure that Orpheus will remain financially, organizationally, and artistically viable over the long run.

The board officially defines and safeguards our mission, exercises fiduciary responsibility, oversees administrative management, and acts as a critical link between Orpheus and the community. In 1998, we added musicians to the board in order to deepen the connection between the orchestra's organizational and creative decisions. With elected representatives on the board, every member of the orchestra knows that no aspect of the organization is "off limits." The musicians have full access to information concerning our plans and operations, and they are directly involved in the most sensitive decisions regarding budgets, finances, product development, and strategic planning.

We have also discovered that adding musicians to the board helps us to recruit new trustees who, as generous volunteers, are in constant demand by Orpheus—and our competitors. The opportunity to sit next to great musicians, as well as top business leaders, has proven to be a powerful tool for building Orpheus's board, and our entire organization benefits.

Management, our twelve-member administrative team, is responsible for running the business and we have broad authority to perform our duties independent of the day-to-day supervision or approval of the board. That covers a lot of ground, since each year we develop and implement a complex operating plan covering more than one hundred events. For example, during the 1999–2000 season, Orpheus produced a five-concert subscription series at Carnegie Hall; performed more than sixty concerts in cities throughout North America, Europe, and Asia; participated in national television and radio broadcasts experienced by more than 8 million people; recorded or released five new CDs; and taught more than twenty-five hundred public school students in New York City.

Each year, the musicians elect three members to participate in the management team. As "artistic directors," their primary role is to propose and develop future projects, ideas, and initiatives, working closely with me to shape the orchestra's products and services through a process of collaboration and consent. This structure also assures informal musician involvement in many areas of Orpheus, and we encourage everyone on the administrative team to seek input from members of the orchestra on all of their projects. Though a new marketing person might be surprised to learn that she is expected to consult a clarinet player about how to plan an Orpheus subscription brochure, she soon learns that musicians—who perform in front of thousands of people at Orpheus concerts, night after night—often have valuable insight into how people respond to the orchestra, and why.

J. P. MORGAN CHASE & COMPANY: MAKING DECISIONS WHERE THE CUSTOMERS ARE

Firms that specialize in global financial transactions live in a complex environment that is heavily regulated, both by internal management controls and by external laws and statutes. But, while the natural tendency within such firms might be to enforce strong limits to employee authority, some have found that empowering individual workers, as we do in Orpheus, can enhance their capacity to successfully and efficiently manage complexity while creating a sense of employee "ownership."

As one of the oldest and most prestigious banks in the world, J. P. Morgan & Company set the trends that others in the financial services industry followed for more than a century. Founded in 1861 by J. Pierpont Morgan, the firm financed and helped build some of America's most important companies, including U.S. Steel, General Electric, American Telephone & Telegraph (AT&T), and many others. Although government legislation after the stock market crash of 1929 required J. P. Morgan to spin off the investment banking side of the business (forming Morgan Stanley in the process) J. P. Morgan & Company continued to thrive and grow.

J. P. Morgan's good fortunes took a sharp downward turn in the mid-1990s, however, as a flurry of mergers and acquisitions in the financial sector created increasingly larger institutions offering broader ranges of products and services. As Morgan turned down potential mergers with Citibank (which went on to become a part of Citigroup, Inc.), Merrill Lynch & Company, and Dean Witter (which later merged with Morgan Stanley to create Morgan Stanley Dean Witter), its share price began to fall behind other securities firms. In 1999, Wall Street punished the firm as shares fell 12 percent from May through the end of the year. During this same period, Goldman Sachs Group's shares rose 35 percent, and Morgan Stanley's shares increased 37 percent.[5]

Potential deals with a variety of financial institutions, including Goldman Sachs, HSBC Holdings PLC, Travelers Corporation, First Union Corporation, Deutsche Bank, and others, were explored; as each fell through for one reason or another, J. P. Morgan's management felt increasing pressure to find a partner and make a deal on its own terms, before the company was forced to accept an unfavorable takeover.

In 2000, Chase Manhattan agreed to acquire J. P. Morgan in a stock swap valued at the time at $30 billion. At the time of the merger with Chase Manhattan, J. P. Morgan & Company offered a full range of commercial banking and investment services internationally, including banking, financial advisory, securities underwriting, trading, and investment fund management services. In fiscal year 1999 the company saw revenues of $18.1 billion and employed more than fifteen thousand people. With more than ninety thousand people located in sixty different countries around the world, the newly formed J. P. Morgan Chase & Company ranked as the second-largest bank in the United States.

Though there were a variety of reasons why Chase Manhattan was interested in acquiring J. P. Morgan—including its venerable name, rich history, and sterling roster of clients—one key factor was the Morgan "culture" of developing long-term relationships with clients, built on a tradition of impeccable and responsive service.

A Flat Organization

Banks and financial institutions have traditionally reveled in hierarchies and ironclad central control. One of premerger J. P. Morgan's hallmarks was its decentralized organization that allowed decisions to be made where the customers were, no matter where in the world they might be. Morgan's approach stood in stark contrast to the multiple layers of supervisors, branch managers, district managers, assistant vice presidents, vice presidents, and senior vice presidents typically involved in the decision-making process at Morgan's competitors.

J. P. Morgan has taken a radically different approach to their organizational chart, one that mirrors Orpheus's in some important ways. Instead of endless layers of management separating clients from the very employees who can make decisions on their behalf, J. P. Morgan's flat organizational structure allows only four levels of employees worldwide: managing directors, vice presidents, associates, and analysts. But, while Morgan's formal, title-based hierarchy is already fairly flat, the organization's *real* hierarchy is often much flatter. According to Claus Loewe, managing director of J. P. Morgan Chase's operation in Frankfurt, Germany, "In many cases, the actual hierarchy of reporting lines is down to two or three, not four. In this office, there is a management committee, and there are certain team leaders, and then the rest of the organization—that's as flat as it comes."

With fewer lines of reporting, employees have a greater voice in how they get their jobs done. Says Oliver Bender, an associate in the London office, "I have a certain framework, and within that framework I have a lot of freedom in what I can do and what I would like to do. And even if it's not within my framework, people will still listen to me and consider my opinions because they value my contribution."

J. P. Morgan Chase maintains a flat hierarchy that cuts across the entire company, and individual business units are vested with great autonomy. Says Loewe, "The management committee represents all of the businesses that we have in Germany, plus what we call a chief operating officer whose job is to look after our mid- and back-office operations. Each of the members of the management committee runs his own business in a very autonomous way."

Serving Clients with Authority

In Germany, J. P. Morgan Chase GmbH handles four separate and distinct lines of business: corporate finance (providing funds for business growth through loans and other debt instruments), risk management (helping clients understand, measure, and manage financial risk in their various business endeavors), underwriting (advising clients on fixed-income and equity transactions), and private banking (discretionary asset management and advising clients on specific investment strategies). In each of these lines of business, except private banking where the company deals with individuals directly, J. P. Morgan Chase's clients are institutional, meaning governments and government agencies, financial institutions (such as insurance companies and asset managers), and industrial corporations. J. P. Morgan Chase developed three policies for putting power in the hands of their employees, in each of these business lines:

1. The company grants its employees extensive autonomy vis-à-vis their own client strategies, while expecting their employees to take responsibility for achieving the organization's goals. According to Claus Loewe, "The guy who runs, for example, a markets business here, and who therefore deals with all of the investor clients in the German market, has complete freedom in terms of how he invests his resources—where he spends his time and how he focuses his team." As a part of granting employees power, J. P. Morgan Chase expects them to meet certain clearly identified and commonly shared targets including "share of wallet" (the percentage of a client's assets under J. P. Morgan Chase control), economic value added,

and new client acquisitions. Once an employee agrees to the targets for a specific year, they are made a part of the employee's plan, and he or she has complete freedom to decide how to reach those objectives. According to Jörn Caumanns, an analyst in the Frankfurt office of J. P. Morgan, "I have a senior banker who tells me which clients we want to target. How I achieve these targets is more or less up to me." This flexibility allows employees to make decisions as they interact with clients, resulting in increased responsiveness. Continues Caumanns, "The client gets answers quicker because they don't have to run through the entire organization."

2. J. P. Morgan Chase grants its employees wide-ranging autonomy to pick and choose from among the company's many different products, which are increasingly international, super-regional, or global, and to determine how they are presented and sold to clients. Although employees can't randomly create new products—this would quickly lead to chaos—they are encouraged to find the right product mix for each of their clients. To do this well, employees must develop extensive knowledge of J. P. Morgan Chase's products, both in and beyond their office. The right mix, for example, might include an equity product in Germany and an entirely different product out of London. Employees operate within the guidelines of the products—size, risk and returns, thresholds and caps—but they solely determine how to apply them to each client's needs.
3. J. P. Morgan Chase provides its employees with the power of information through its Intranet and other technology tools. By gathering all of the company's analytical tools, transaction history, and product information, and making this information available globally and immediately, Morgan gives its employees greater ability to respond to client needs quickly, locally, and autonomously. Information systems and processes remove the limitations of geography and time, while creating a discipline in the organization's processes for clearing transactions, transferring monies, supporting client transactions, and other business. The power of information has also created a new kind of hierarchy within J. P. Morgan Chase, based on knowledge and experience. You won't find this hierarchy on any

organization chart, but it's one that has become increasingly important to the company. At Morgan, information helps break down the formal walls that often separate offices from one another, and encourages employees to create their own teams and affiliations to respond to client needs. Says Claus Loewe, "If we have a client who requires a specific solution, for example, to raise money in Latin America, then we try to identify the person who best understands that region and another person who best understands the client. We will put them together in the team and they will run the entire transaction, creating a certain transaction-related hierarchy for a limited period of time. But, as employees go through this process on a regular basis, people quickly realize where the knowledge is. The result is an informal knowledge hierarchy that can be tapped to improve their performance and their response to clients." In this system based on knowledge and experience there is no senior, and there is no junior—there are only "knows" and "need to knows." Says Jörn Caumanns, "You're working in project teams consisting of managing directors, associates, and analysts, and everybody has a specific role. Working in teams with all levels of employees brings down the hierarchies you may have felt beforehand."

Tearing Down Walls

Of course, every organization has its formal and informal boundaries, and J. P. Morgan Chase is no different. Managing directors, for example, tend to spend a lot of their time communicating within their own community of managing directors; some may find it hard to pick up the phone or to go over and talk to an analyst, who may, in turn, find it difficult to simply walk into a managing director's office and speak his or her mind.

But J. P. Morgan Chase has taken a variety of steps to break down these natural interpersonal barriers and to open up a free exchange of information across the corporation, regardless of position and rank, to support the company's culture of collegiality, teamwork, and camaraderie. For example, managing directors invite small groups of analysts, vice presidents, and other employees to join them for breakfast to discuss important business issues in a relaxed environment, breaking down hierarchical boundaries and encouraging people to get to know each other and work together. Informal get-togethers and receptions create an "equality of ideas" and foster the kind of environment where people aren't afraid to cross organizational lines to accomplish their goals.

Senior members of the J. P. Morgan team make a point of involving junior employees in meetings, building their presentation skills and self-confidence in the process. Says Oliver Bender, "We have a regular Monday lunch meeting where people explain what's going on and the project leaders and the managing directors give a quick summary of what happened last week and what's going to happen this week. They often delegate this task to the associates in their teams to give them a platform to speak." Junior employees are also routinely brought along to client presentation meetings, even for the firm's most senior and most important clients. These employees have a unique opportunity to learn and to observe, and they are often able to add value to meetings when details are discussed that they were involved in preparing. The relationships that they inevitably form with clients serve them—and the firm—well.

Premerger J. P. Morgan twice landed on *Fortune* magazine's list of the "50 Best Companies for Minorities," and Morgan employees consistently report that they feel both challenged and rewarded in their jobs. According to Jörn Caumanns, the autonomy allowed him by J. P. Morgan is one of the key reasons for his long tenure with the firm. Says Caumanns, "I always thought this was the right job. A year ago, the responsibility and the independence that you were given at a New Economy company was unparalleled, but I feel more valuable here." Adds Oliver Bender, "Money is an important aspect of business life, but money doesn't compensate for a miserable life where you never see a client and never see the impact of your work. At

J. P. Morgan, you have freedom of mind and freedom of speech and you can actually see what's happening with the work you're producing. It motivates me because I know that ultimately I'm more than a little wheel in a big machine."

PUTTING THIS PRINCIPLE INTO PRACTICE

Creating an environment where employees are truly empowered means loosening the reins on authority and giving employees access to resources that are usually controlled by managers. You may meet resistance from supervisors who believe they have earned a "turnkey" position—but the trust you give to and gain from employees at every level will garner better products and happier customers.

Five Steps for Loosening the Reins of Power

STEP 1: **Encourage decision making by *all* employees, not just a select few.** There are leaders and followers in every organization; the key is to ensure that these roles don't get frozen in place. To accomplish this, delegate decision-making authority down to the lowest level possible, allow front-line workers to respond directly to customers and clients without constantly seeking management approval, and give employees at every level leadership opportunities that are built—even temporarily—into their job descriptions and backed up by decision-making authority. To allow employees to develop decision-making skills without being overwhelmed, consider assigning projects and tasks that allow workers to gradually build their leadership muscles. Examples might include studying a business opportunity or problem and presenting a proposal to top management, organizing a company event, launching a new customer-service initiative, or chairing an interdepartmental committee. One excellent example is W. L. Gore and Associates, where the so-called waterline principle encourages associates to make most routine decisions on their own, but protects Gore's overall position by requiring associates to consult with others when a decision could adversely affect the company's reputation or financial stability.

STEP 2: Delegate tasks and authority widely. Sometimes it takes a life-changing event to help one realize the importance of delegating tasks and authority to employees. Linda Ellerbee, journalist and CEO of Lucky Duck Productions, tells this story: "My biggest mistake as a manager was holding control too tightly. When I started Lucky Duck Productions in 1987, I had no management experience. As a consequence, I did what many people who are new at running their own companies do: I wanted to be involved in every detail of the business at all times. I literally wanted to go into the editing room and cut every piece myself. We ran our company that way for nearly five years. Then, in 1992, I was diagnosed with cancer. The timing couldn't have been worse. We had just gotten our first really big project—to produce a news series for kids on Nickelodeon cable. So the day after I was diagnosed, I called in the entire staff, told them that I had cancer, and basically asked if they could try to hold things together until I was ready to take over again. And for months I wasn't well. But I learned a valuable lesson. I had hired really good people who were good at their jobs, and what they needed was for me to get out of their way. The company continued to thrive in my absence. I never tried to micromanage again."[6]

STEP 3: Involve employees in determining the company's and their own goals. Employees who are involved in creating an organization's goals will feel invested in them, and will be much more likely to meet them. Since the beginning, Austin, Texas–based Whole Foods, pioneer of the natural foods supermarket concept, has made a point of involving employees, known by the company as "team members," in the development and periodic review of the organization's mission and core values. The Whole Foods mission statement, dubbed the Declaration of Interdependence, was originally created by sixty Whole Foods employees in 1985 and has been updated three times since then. Key to the Whole Foods mission is the belief that the company should exist not only to make a profit but also to serve its stakeholders: its customers, employees, investors, the environment, and the community. The result is a company that is the nation's number one natural foods chain in sales with annual revenue in excess of $1.5 billion.[7]

STEP 4: Open up your books to all employees. At medical supplies distributor Physician's Sales and Service, Inc. (PSS), of Jacksonville, Florida, CEO Pat Kelly has long been a believer in the benefit of opening the books to all employees. The company's financials are not simply shared with employees, they are literally plastered all over the walls of PSS's branch offices, which serve more than ninety thousand physicians' practices nationwide. Key financial data, including sales and gross margin per person and branch performance against financial targets, are shared with employees on a daily, weekly, and monthly basis, and employees take ownership for the numbers, the results they represent, and the refining of their work as needed. Founded in 1983, PSS has quickly grown into the nation's largest medical supplier to physicians, with annual sales in excess of $1.7 billion.[8]

STEP 5: Create self-managing work teams (and stay out of the way). Teams that put real power and authority in the hands of employees can be a very powerful force within an organization. At General Electric's jet-engine assembly facility in Durham, North Carolina, self-managing work teams are the norm, not the exception. The members of these teams have unprecedented levels of authority and responsibility for determining how, when, and where they will do their jobs. Says technician Duane Williams, "We had to come up with our own schedule. We had the chance to order tools, tool carts, and so on. We had to figure out how the assembly line to make the engine should flow. We were put on councils for every part of the business. I was never valued that much as an employee in my life. I had never been at the point where I couldn't wait to get to work. But here, I couldn't wait to get to work every day. That's no BS."[9] These self-managing teams have an extraordinary track record of finding ways to build better products more efficiently than ever before.

Potential Traps and Landmines

- **Delegating authority without putting appropriate feedback mechanisms into place.** Delegating authority is more than just the best way to put power in the hands of the people doing the work; it is also a particularly effective way for managers to leverage their own efforts and increase their productivity. However, delegated authority without feedback mechanisms can quickly lead to disaster, especially if workers find themselves too far down the wrong path and fail to seek help when serious problems arise. Proper delegation involves more than just giving employees authority; it also requires setting up appropriate mechanisms for obtaining and integrating feedback, such as milestones, regular progress reports, status meetings, and other methods of communication. The best tools provide exactly the quantity of genuinely valuable information managers and other employees need, at a frequency that doesn't lead to employees spending more time preparing reports or attending meetings than doing their jobs.
- **Managers who delegate responsibility for certain jobs, projects, and tasks, but not the authority necessary to get them done.** Delegating tasks and responsibility requires managers to let go of a certain amount of personal and organizational power, and many managers simply lack the confidence and experience to delegate effectively. Proper delegation requires a grant of authority as well as responsibility; anything less will lead to worker frustration when others in the organization impede their efforts or simply refuse to cooperate. Assign authority (to make decisions, direct financial and other resources, and so forth) when delegating responsibility, and invite your employees to ask for more if they need it. Remember that in new workplace situations, managers are just as likely to need training and support as employees are. In spite of the advantages of delegating authority, many managers will find it difficult to delegate.
- **Forgetting that old habits die hard, and that it is far more difficult to undo years of hierarchy than you think.** It's easy to say that every manager and every organization should put power in the hands of the

people doing the work, but for many companies evolutionary rather than revolutionary change offers the best course. Consider gradually increasing the scope of authority given to workers, while simultaneously fostering the confidence of managers in the abilities of their employees. Developing a culture of trust requires everyone in the company to buy into the process, from the very top level of management to front-line workers. To underscore the company's commitment to empowerment, make delegating authority part of every supervisor's performance rating, and be sure to provide training in effective delegation. The transition will take time.

- **Workers who do not take responsibility for the impact of their decisions.** With worker empowerment, decisions get made closer to customers and clients by the employees who know them best, and workers become progressively more competent and capable as they make decisions on their own. Remember, though, that worker empowerment only succeeds if employees assume personal responsibility for following through on assigned duties and for the decisions they make. Companies have to hold their workers to a high standard of accountability; workers must hold themselves to an equally high standard. This doesn't mean punishing workers whenever they drop the ball, but it does mean helping them learn from their mistakes and giving them the training and support they need to do the job right the next time.

Putting power in the hands of the people doing the work is at the very heart of the Orpheus Process, and this principle forms the foundation for all others. Many of Orpheus's and J. P. Morgan Chase's successes can be traced to empowering employees, trusting and allowing them to make creative decisions, and giving them authority to use their knowledge and skills.

3

Encourage Individual Responsibility for Product and Quality

Good, better, best
Never let it rest
Until the good becomes the better
And the better becomes the best.

—CHILDREN'S RHYME

Strong leadership is justifiably considered an essential ingredient of successful companies, but when leadership is invested in only one person or a select few it's only natural that the vast majority of employees feel less than personally responsible for producing high-quality products and services. We've seen how empowerment can be a valuable tool for engaging employees in company decisions and their outcomes. But putting power in the hands of the people doing the work will yield little benefit—and risk much harm—to companies that fail to also encourage personal responsibility for product and quality among all their employees. In the final analysis, individuals taking responsibility for a company's products and services allow companies to successfully meet their goals.

In most companies, every time a supervisor or manager assigns an employee a task, that employee faces a critical choice: either to take personal responsibility for the successful completion of the task, or to avoid it.

Orpheus members have no such choice. Since our orchestra has no conductor, each individual member is directly and personally responsible for the quality of our performances. There's no one to hide behind or to pass the buck to. Speaking to any member of Orpheus yields a common refrain: "I feel responsible for ensuring that our concerts aren't just good, or even great, but that they're as close to perfection as possible."

The quality of our products effects our bottom line, just like in any other company. The business implications are clear: Product excellence garners glowing reviews and publicity, driving up ticket sales and record sales and generating tour bookings and broadcasting opportunities. Everyone in our organization takes personal responsibility for product and quality, and constantly strives to deliver the best musical product possible.

THE PRINCIPLE

Orchestral musicians inhabit a professional world where individual initiative carries great risk and offers little potential for reward. In most orchestras, the idea of musicians being allowed to make choices that would significantly affect the quality or character of a musical performance is simply unthinkable. The conductor runs the show and, every night, before thousands of people, he inspires or cajoles the musicians under his baton into expressing his own personal vision of the music. While the best conductors function as catalysts that help individual players reach their highest levels of performance, even the most motivational conductor gives individual musicians little opportunity to shape the product and its quality, other than by following orders.

On the rare occasions when a player-originated idea does find its way into performance, the credit inevitably goes to the conductor. Critics and commentators who write about Leonard Bernstein's performances of Mahler or "Levine's" Beethoven usually make only passing reference to the orchestras that actually perform these works and rarely, if ever, mention any of the individual musicians. Not surprisingly, orchestral musicians often feel detached from the outcome of their own performance. Players in conducted orchestras have no choice but to cede their responsibility for what is in effect someone else's musical product, and they have little incentive, or opportunity, to take responsibility for its quality.

Unfortunately, too many companies operate with this same philosophy. Employees are expected to apply a narrow set of skills to a business plan that is developed from above, with little or no input from them, and consequently little or no ownership. Receptionists, cashiers, and clerks—among a company's lowest-level and lowest-paid employees—know a great deal about a company's customers and make a significant impact on customer satisfaction, revenues, and profits. Yet managers rarely solicit their opinions about improving the company's product and quality because they underestimate the knowledge that these employees bring to their jobs.

In all companies, but especially knowledge-based ones, every employee has the capacity to enhance the organization's commitment to product and quality. When employees at all levels take individual responsibility for achieving their company's business goals, the entire organization inevitably becomes much more productive and effective. Companies that reward employees for taking on and fulfilling individual responsibility for product and quality also significantly increase their ability to attract and retain the best talent. In fact, organizations that successfully encourage individual employees to take responsibility for product and quality can expect:

- Increased worker engagement in their jobs
- Increased ability to delegate decision making
- Increased employee satisfaction and loyalty

In this chapter, we'll explore exactly how we at Orpheus foster individual responsibility and how financial services firm Morgan Stanley invests its workers with personal accountability, leading to customer and client experiences that are unequaled in our industries.

ORPHEUS: A PERSONAL RESPONSIBILITY FOR THE CREATIVE PRODUCT

Orpheus's approach to employee responsibility assumes that every employee brings valuable knowledge to our business decisions, and our conductorless structure requires that each one of our members takes full responsibility for shaping the content and improving the quality of our performances. There is simply no alternative. As board chairman Gonzalo de Las Heras puts it: "Our musicians have to figure out how all the pieces fit together because there's no conductor to tell them. And they also feel responsible for the quality—not only for their own playing, but that of the others."

The enormous power of individuals to shape our organization's outcomes is linked to—and predicated upon—the obligation of individuals to take a substantial measure of personal responsibility for the success of our whole group's performance. If an Orpheus concert is great, then each musician knows that he or she played a vital role in making it great; if the performance is poor, then each member knows that he or she played a role in that outcome as well.

At every stage of rehearsal and performance, our musicians have to be deeply engaged in their own parts *and* aware of the thousands of things that are going on around them so they can simultaneously evaluate the mix, balance, and direction of the entire group. Each player, of course, is responsible for his or her individual performance and constantly strives to meet the technical demands of the music. At the same time, he or she is also taking personal responsibility for the outcome of the group effort, giving painstaking attention to the thousands of details that ultimately shape the design and interpretation of a musical program. On yet another level, the same musicians are also responsible for selecting team leaders and offering suggestions and criticism to help them to bring forth the very best ideas and energies of the group.

Responsibility Leads to Productivity

In analyzing a Gallup Organization survey of more than 1 million employees, Curt Coffman, Gallup's global practice leader, identified twelve workplace characteristics that lead to high levels of worker loyalty and performance. According to Coffman, the most productive firms create a work environment based on employee accountability, and half of his "Q^{12}" characteristics specifically describe individual responsibility for product and quality:

- Employees' job responsibilities are tied to the company's overall purpose and goals.
- Employees know what is expected of them.
- Employees are committed to doing quality work.
- Employees have the opportunity to exercise their expertise every day.
- Employees have the materials and equipment they need to do their work well.
- Employees' opinions can influence decisions.

Coffman estimates that 15 to 25 percent of employees do not want larger responsibility for a company's product and quality, and worse, often resist accountability for their own job responsibilities. But, by putting such conditions in place, a company can improve its products and services and increase customer satisfaction since the majority of workers are eager to take more individual responsibility for product and quality.[1]

Similarly, in his classic business book, *Moments of Truth,* Jan Carlzon, former president of Scandinavian Airlines System (SAS), describes the effect that seemingly "impossible" goals or standards can have in galvanizing employee responsibility. When Carlzon took over the reins of SAS, the company was facing the deregulation of the U.S. airline industry, dramatic increases in global competition, a worldwide fuel crisis that was driving up operating costs, and years of bureaucratic inertia within the organization.

Carlzon responded to these challenges by shifting the company's product philosophy from flying airplanes to flying people and making SAS employees directly responsible for meeting the needs of SAS's customers. Carlzon identifies four points as the foundation of his pioneering approach to fostering a culture of individual responsibility:

- Every employee needs to know and feel that he is needed.
- Every employee wants to be treated as an individual.
- Giving an employee the freedom to take responsibility releases resources that would otherwise remain concealed.
- An individual without information cannot take responsibility; an individual who is given information cannot help but take responsibility.[2]

One of Carlzon's key initiatives was a "punctuality" campaign, designed to ensure that SAS flights would take off on time—a fairly rare occurrence when he first took the helm. Says Carlzon, "The punctuality campaign's most important achievement was rallying everyone at SAS behind the same objective. Our former target had been that 80 percent of the planes would depart on time. This gave everybody an escape valve: 20 percent of the planes were allowed to be late, so what difference would it make if they didn't hurry to make sure *their* flight was on time? Now the target was 100 percent. With no further directives from top management, everyone tried to work a little more smoothly and efficiently. Punctuality had become a group concern. Before, nobody was responsible. Now, everyone was."[3]

In their book, *First, Break All the Rules: What the World's Greatest Managers Do Differently*, Curt Coffman and his colleague Marcus Buckingham explain that another key to encouraging employees to take individual responsibility is defining the "right" outcomes, and then allowing each employee to find his or her route to productive accomplishment. According to Coffman and Buckingham, "Great managers want each employee to feel a certain tension, a tension to achieve. Defining the right outcomes creates that tension. By defining, and more often than not, measuring the required outcomes, great managers create an environment where each employee feels that little thrill of pressure, that sense of being out there by oneself with a very definite target."[4]

In Orpheus, the responsibility each one of our members takes for achieving our desired objectives plays an especially important role when we are faced with less-than-perfect circumstances. Rather than going through the motions in poor conditions, our members feel responsible for digging in and working even harder, increasing their energy and concentration to ensure that our goals for product excellence are met. Says violinist Ronnie Bauch, "When performance conditions are poor, you can feel as if you have created a beautiful and wonderful product, and it has been put in a torn cardboard box. But we all know we can turn that around, and we do."

Striving to Achieve the Highest Standards

In Orpheus, we also go a step further by first sharing the authority to define the right outcomes among all our employees, and then encouraging each individual in the organization to aim high. Every one of our musicians constantly takes responsibility for the overall quality of our product by fighting for what he or she believes is the right way to approach musical issues.

To cite one example, in 1999 we were preparing for a Carnegie Hall concert with a renowned guest soloist, mezzo-soprano Lorraine Hunt Lieberson. During the run-through rehearsal, a single person, taking responsibility, defined the "right" outcome at the highest standard: bassoonist Frank Morelli, who felt that the violins weren't doing enough in the opening of an aria by George Friedrich Handel to frame Lieberson's dynamic and emotional range.

From his perch in the back of the wind section, Morelli described and demonstrated on his instrument the hushed quality he was after. The violins tried it again. The result was better, but Morelli thought that the moment could be even more dramatic, so he challenged the section to produce an extremely soft but expressive sound. Some of the violins began to grumble, but by now other members of the orchestra were voicing their support for the idea. There was real tension in the orchestra when Morelli pushed his colleagues to achieve more. Finally, with one more try, the violins achieved what they, and everyone else in the group, enthusiastically agreed was a striking, original, and highly effective result, one that received a great response from the audience that evening. In the best Orpheus tradition, Morelli also gave credit to the people who actively put his standard into action.

In a traditional management hierarchy, employees who have specialized expertise can feel restrained from sharing such innovative ideas that reach beyond their primary responsibilities. As a wind player, Morelli had relatively little understanding how difficult it might be for the string players to realize the effect he sought—but he was also not inhibited by his narrow technical knowledge of the issues involved. Rather than focusing only on his own performance, he took responsibility for the music and its impact on the audience. By giving every member of Orpheus equal and individual responsibility for our overall product and quality, we consistently achieve the highest standards of performance.

Learning from Mistakes and Taking Risks

In many organizations, the response to failure is an official "lessons-learned" meeting, where the responsible manager itemizes the mistakes that were made and retrospectively identifies the proper solutions.

In Orpheus, we take a different approach, based on the reality that no organization—including ours—can ever be error-free. Since our members feel (and in fact, are) directly responsible for product and quality, they are highly motivated to learn from their mistakes, and they strive especially hard to do a better job the next time. (Our emphasis on good communication and consensus-building, which will be discussed in chapters 7 and 8, also allow us to bypass blame assessment and focus on improving future performance.) Observes violinist Martha Caplin, a member of Orpheus since 1982, "If the product doesn't turn out well, that's when you learn what works and what doesn't work. Our performances are part of the ongoing learning process." This attitude plays a powerful role in making Orpheus a forward-looking organization.

Orpheus has no one person who decides what lessons we need to learn from our failures; any person can and will take responsibility for improving our performance and addressing problems. We are all constantly communicating with one another, actively trying to improve the organization by learning from our mistakes, and we rotate and share the responsibility for identifying recurring issues. When a problem proves to be recurring, any member can call a meeting that functions much like a rehearsal, with everyone in the group taking an active role in trying to understand the issues and solve the problem. While everyone in Orpheus has a strong interest in avoiding failure, our organization considers learning, rather than punishment, to be the correct response to mistakes. Consequently, we do not allow problem solving to degenerate into finger-pointing.

When an organization makes risk avoidance its paramount value, its products quickly become predictable. For an orchestra, predictable performances spell creative mediocrity and—over time—financial disaster. By constantly reenforcing the distinction between blame assessment and problem solving, we have developed an organizational climate that encourages everyone in Orpheus to take carefully considered risks. This willingness to take risks on new or untested repertoire, performance practices, and interpretations has played a significant and indispensable role in attaining our international reputation for artistic quality and creative innovation.

The first time we ever tried to perform Aaron Copland's *Short Symphony*, the rhythmic complexity of the score proved more than the orchestra could handle; without a conductor, it was impossible for our musicians to follow the overlapping and conflicting rhythms, much less to stay together. When the first full rehearsal collapsed in confusion, the situation was so discouraging that some members even suggested bringing in a conductor to guide the group through rehearsals.

Cellist Eric Bartlett had another idea about how to solve the problem. Drawing on his vast experience with twentieth-century music, Bartlett invested dozens of hours to map out the beats of every rhythmic line in the twelve-hundred-measure piece and created a tape-recorded "click track" for the individual musicians to follow. When the orchestra tried out Bartlett's new invention at the next rehearsal, the results were dramatic and immediate, and the musicians quickly mastered the complexities of Copland's work. The click track became a valuable new tool for solving the difficult rhythmic problems we face when performing modern music, allowing us to expand our repertoire.

In Orpheus, we depend on our members to utilize all of their knowledge and technical expertise when solving problems, and companies that foster a risk-taking environment where employees have the freedom and responsibility to explore unconventional solutions outside their primary jobs will see similar benefits in their products and performance.

The Rewards of Excellence

Companies cannot simply push responsibility downward and expect employees to automatically accept the change and improve their performance as a result. According to Edward Lawler, director of the Center for Effective Organizations at the University of Southern California, employees are unlikely to take on increased individual responsibility unless they also feel a sense of psychological "ownership" of the organization.

For employees in any organization to take responsibility for its products and quality, they have to have a stake in the outcome. In numerous studies, Lawler has documented the importance of sharing information, knowledge, power, and rewards at all levels. Companies that attempt to foster individual responsibility in the workforce, but fail to invest in employees in this way, risk stagnating, and even declining, levels of performance. Says Lawler, flattening the organizational hierarchy "is just one leg of the stool. All it does is move power downward, and power without information, knowledge, and rewards is absolutely dangerous. . . . Most Fortune 1000 companies still do not give basic financial information to most of their employees. They do not get an annual report, they do not get invited to meetings which describe the economic performance of the organization, either at the local business unit level or at the corporate level." Furthermore, says Lawler, "In the area of rewards, most employees are not covered by any kind of meaningful profit-sharing plan, employee ownership plan, or gain-sharing plan. Most have very limited power."[5]

Does ownership, particularly in the form of an equity stake, lead to bottom-line improvements? In a study of corporate survival rates, Rutgers professors Douglas Kruse and Joseph Blasi, and Margaret Blair of the Brookings Institute, discovered that companies where employees own at least 20 percent of the company's stock are significantly less likely to go bankrupt or be acquired than companies without employee ownership. Says Kruse, "On average, an employee-owned company is 4 to 5 percent more productive than a comparable company that isn't employee-owned."[6]

At Unilever's soap powder plant in Cartersville, Georgia, home of such familiar brands as Wisk, All, and Surf, a company goal-sharing plan encouraged employees to develop new ways to work more efficiently by giving them half of the company's first-year savings from employee innovations. When the plan went into effect, management was flooded with cost-saving and money-making ideas. In a recent year, goal-sharing payments amounted to $4,900 for each plant worker.[7]

Although Orpheus, as a not-for-profit, doesn't provide employees with stock options, we do offer our members two forms of ownership that few other organizations can match, and that represent a stake-holding structure unequaled in our field:

- As long as they remain active and engaged participants, our members cannot be fired. Like tenured professors, they are members for life, if they so choose.
- Everything our members do to strengthen the orchestra's strategy directly benefits each individual, because the organization is committed to investing surpluses in equitably distributed increased compensation to the people who create our products.

Freed from fear of losing their jobs if they speak their minds and encouraged by the very real impact they can have on the organization and the quality of its products, our musicians willingly take on extraordinary levels of individual responsibility. Time and again, I have seen our musicians go far beyond conventional expectations in order to do everything in their power to improve our musical product and enhance our profile and revenues.

MORGAN STANLEY: ONE STEP AHEAD OF THE COMPETITION

As we've seen, our organization relies on individual employees taking responsibility for constantly improving the quality of our products and our financial performance. But can this principle apply in an industry where competitive and regulatory pressures seem to limit employees' abilities to shape a company's product?

Few businesses are more conservative, and regulated, than old-line investment banks. Although many still depend on a traditional management hierarchy to run their day-to-day operations, at least one firm has broken this mold, giving individual employees wide-ranging responsibility and authority to meet and exceed customer expectations on a regular basis.

With fiscal year 2000 revenues of $45.4 billion—up 30 percent from fiscal year 1999's figure of $34.9 billion—and net income of $5.5 billion, Morgan Stanley is one of the world's top financial services firms. A leader in investment banking with $5 billion in investment banking revenues in 2000, it is the second-ranked retail broker by financial advisers in the United States and one of the top on-line brokers. The firm is a leader in asset management and its Discover credit card is ranked third after Visa and MasterCard. With more than sixty thousand employees working in six hundred offices, operating in twenty-seven different countries, and managing $502 billion in assets, Morgan Stanley's reach is global and its resources and depth of experience profound.

The Electronic Office

In today's business environment, corporate processes cannot afford to be static. As new products are developed, and new methods and technologies are implemented to provide them to clients and customers, customer demands constantly shift and companies have to keep up with these changes to remain effective. The best firms address current customer needs while also anticipating, and building operations around, customers' expectations in the future.

In 1993, when the Internet was still a matter of peripheral concern for most nontechnology corporations, a small group of Morgan Stanley employees began to articulate a vision that the Internet had the potential to transform business communications. These employees—including Jon Saxe, Don Callahan, Marc Donner, Andy Lowry, Nicky Rungunasen, Ben Fried,

Mark Kennedy, and others—took personal responsibility for making this vision a reality at Morgan Stanley.

In 1993, Marc Donner, vice president (now principal) of EBusiness Technology for Morgan Stanley, was given an assignment: completely automate the firm by making paper-based transactions a thing of the past. Donner, however, considered the pursuit of a "paperless office" a dead end for the firm and, rather than spend company time and resources on a limited objective, he suggested a more ambitious endeavor, which he termed the Electronic Office. Donner hired a group of half a dozen talented systems people to help define and build the Electronic Office and quickly got to work.

At the heart of their concept was a then-new technology called Mosaic, the revolutionary Internet browser developed in 1992 by Marc Andreessen at the University of Illinois at Urbana-Champaign's National Center for Supercomputing Applications (NCSA). Says Donner, "I had been an Internet hound since during my grad school time, and I had been involved in TCP/IP and Internet technology ever since—by now a long, long time. So we pulled in the Mosaic browser, the NCSA server, and the CERN server as source code, because that was the only way to get it, and then we put up Web servers all over the firm. We went live on the Fourth of July 1994 in our Fixed Income Division."

Donner's Electronic Office group had created the world's first Intranet through the implementation of Internet technology within Morgan Stanley. By 1994, Morgan Stanley had ninety Web servers powering its Intranet, and the firm attracted the attention of Netscape, which eventually selected Morgan Stanley to take it public in 1995. The Netscape IPO set records, turning cofounder Jim Clark into a billionaire and many Netscape employees into instant millionaires, and touched off the Internet revolution that swept the nation.

Today the power of Internet technology to change the way people do business day to day has been amply demonstrated, but in the mid-1990s such thinking was revolutionary. Not surprisingly, even as the Electronic Office was up and running and beginning to prove its worth, some forces within the firm were arrayed against it. Says Donner, "There was tremendous resistance internally—from the Information Technology (IT) department, not from the business people. In their minds, this was technology for its own sake. It wasn't saving money, and it wasn't providing any specific business functionality, so people were very skeptical of it. Our challenge was to articulate the value of the technology as an information-sharing tool."

Marc Donner continued to push hard for his personal vision of the Electronic Office, taking personal responsibility for ensuring Morgan Stanley's primacy in the fast-moving world of Internet technology. To achieve the firm's goals, the Electronic Office group was broken down into three separate units. One was given the assignment to build infrastructure (Web servers, composition and production tools), the second unit was given the task of developing Web delivery software applications, and the third was charged with creating platforms to deliver information to the outside world through the Internet. This project, later named ClientLink, became a highly effective tool for developing closer relationships with the firm's clients and again set the standard for the rest of the industry.

Core Responsibilities

When the group of employees spun off from the Electronic Office project was charged with the task of creating a platform for delivery of information to the outside world, it was already clear that the best way to do this would be through the Internet. What was not clear, however, was exactly what information would be presented and what format this presentation should take. Defining these parameters first required a close look at Morgan Stanley's core competencies.

Says Don Callahan, managing director and director of marketing for institutional securities at Morgan Stanley, "If you consider the core values of the investment banking and securities business, it's about turning data into information, turning that information into knowledge, turning that knowledge into insight, and insight into wisdom. From the Morgan Stanley point of view, instead of wisdom we would like to turn that into an actual trade or other transaction. So the value chain is data being harvested, refined, and then improved upon to a level where we can bring our clients greater insight."

To create ClientLink, Morgan Stanley's proprietary, Web-based system that links the company's prodigious financial information and resources with its clients, individual Morgan Stanley employees once again took personal responsibility for realizing their vision and won approval from Morgan Stanley's operating committee.

First, they built ResearchLink, making Morgan Stanley the first investment firm to digitize its research product. Callahan recalls, "We had a group of developers that recognized that the key to Internet client service was going to be personalization, so they built a set of tools that allowed clients to create crude profiles and specify the information or news they wanted to track." As ResearchLink and ClientLink grew, personalization remained the key. According to Callahan, "We need to deliver ideas that are highly pertinent, and present them in a way that allows clients to get to that next level of depth with a phone conversation with us or a personal interaction. We firmly believe that the human ought to be right in the middle of the process, and that it's all about the quality of the understanding of the individual's needs."

To achieve these goals, Morgan Stanley conducts highly sophisticated database marketing and subsegmentation modeling, and uses inference databases to anticipate client needs—even before clients realize they have them. This gives an account representative the ability to call up clients about matters of very specific interest and say, "I know you've been thinking about this for a while. We really think that now is the right time. Here are the reasons why."

Employees Taking Responsibility

It's not an accident that Morgan Stanley employees enthusiastically embrace taking responsibility on the job. The firm's nonbureaucratic work environment and culture of excellence attracts and rewards talented people who want to take responsibility and who want to work for a firm with few organizational boundaries to limit their success. Morgan Stanley's operations in Japan are a case in point. Commencing operations in Japan in 1970, Morgan Stanley, like other international companies, faced the challenge of becoming fully integrated into the Japanese market. The firm recognized that meeting this challenge would require the ongoing efforts of a talented and dedicated group of employees who would be fully committed to achieving its clients' goals. Says Thierry Porté, president of Morgan Stanley's Institutional Securities operations in Japan, "Our objective has been to set the pace in the industry and become the preeminent financial services firm. From a product standpoint our strength in Japan has been to bring innovations, new products and new ideas to this market, to adapt them in an appropriate way to Japan."

But while having great products has been essential to Morgan Stanley's success in Japan, the trust that it has established with its clients and counterparts is the bedrock of the firm's reputation. This trust stems from its clients' understanding that Morgan Stanley's people put the client first. The ability to build and maintain this trust is derived directly from the firm's culture of excellence, values, and individual responsibility. "Hiring the best and the brightest alone is not enough to build a business," notes Porté. "Yes, you need to create a challenging work environment and provide employees with all the tools and resources necessary to get their jobs done, but ultimately the key to success and trust is the fact that our employees share our core values and culture. Personal integrity, entrepreneurial spirit, and respect for other individuals in the firm are key values that promote a culture in which individuals can be given responsibility and the firm knows they will put clients first. Without these shared values we would not be where we are today."

According to John McGeehan, managing director and chief administrative officer in Japan, Morgan Stanley's unique culture is what originally brought him to the firm in 1988, and it's what continues to attract highly qualified people today. "What attracted me was the firm's unstructured environment and the fact that, assuming I demonstrated the aptitude, I would have the ability to take on a fair amount of responsibility at a relatively young age. When I think about not just creative people, but very self-directed and confident people, that's the kind of environment that they're looking to be a part of, a wide open work space—there's not a lot of middle, not a lot of bureaucracy. I often joke with people about my first day at a sales job at Morgan Stanley. It was a little bit like 'Hey, great to have you on the team. Now, here's a phone book, start at *A*. When you get to *Z*, call me.' That's how much freedom you get. It's a very powerful thing."

But though Morgan Stanley rewards individual achievement, it discourages employees from flaunting their personal successes. There is no star system at Morgan Stanley; employees are expected to keep the interests of the team, the firm, and the client above their own. The firm is acutely aware that it derives its greatest strength from its network of employees, leveraging the depth of experience and knowledge that comes from attracting a diverse group of individuals of different genders, nationalities, educational backgrounds, and experiential skill sets. But the firm also knows that hiring the most talented candidates improves everyone's performance. Says McGeehan, "The challenge of working with other people of similar qualities, people who are highly self-motivated, who work well in an unstructured environment and who are very smart raises your game. It raises everybody's game."

Rewarding employee performance is also an important part of Morgan Stanley's corporate culture. Managers notice when employees take personal initiative to solve client problems and when they provide clients with outstanding service. Says Porté, "As the leader in the industry, we believe we also need to be a leader in terms of the way we reward people. It's very much a performance-based culture, so it is a system that's based on rewarding individual performance while at the same time taking into account their collaborative responsibilities."

But though financial rewards are an important factor for any employee, they are not the main reason that employees choose to work for Morgan Stanley. In surveys of staff in Japan, employees consistently report that compensation and promotions are not the main reason why they chose to work for the firm or why they choose to stay. Instead, employees are loyal to Morgan Stanley because of the large amount of responsibility and trust the firm grants them, and the thrill of working with colleagues who are the best in the industry. In this way, Morgan Stanley's corporate culture perpetuates itself, and it ensures that the firm will always be a force to reckon with in the industry.

PUTTING THIS PRINCIPLE INTO PRACTICE

It's a dangerously short road from employees who take no responsibility for the work of the organization as a whole to a workforce indifferent to the quality of its own work product. Indifference can quickly spread through an unwary organization, making mediocre product quality the accepted norm rather than the rare exception.

But taking responsibility isn't something that a manager or business owner can force employees to do, nor is it something that workers will embrace unless they believe in the company, its products and services, and its ways of doing business—including the way it treats workers, clients, and customers.

Five Steps for Fostering Employee Responsibility

STEP 1: **Give employees leeway to define the "right" outcome.** Employees who have no control over how an organization's products are designed, produced, or marketed are unlikely to go out of their way to take responsibility for quality. Employees working for the Atlanta, Georgia–based Ritz-Carlton Hotel Company are given the responsibility to ensure an exceptional guest experience, backed up by the authority to spend up to $2,000 to resolve a guest complaint, no questions asked.[8]

STEP 2: **Give employees a sense of ownership.** Delphi Automotive Systems Corporation recently redesigned its Oak Creek, Wisconsin, automotive catalytic converter manufacturing plant. Along with the new work environment came a new way of doing business: customer-centered work cells that require large amounts of individual responsibility from members. Cell workers communicate directly with customers, inspect the products they build, take responsibility for the individual parts they work on, measure productivity, and set their own work schedules. Says Mike Kahle, coadministrator of Dephi's Quality Network Suggestion Program and part-time press operator, "I've been here twenty-six years. This place used to be nothing but conveyors—8,000 feet of conveyors. Now it's down to about 200 feet. We've become lean. I run the suggestion program during the week, and I work overtime and weekends as a press operator. That used to mean just running the press. But now press operators have control over the whole operation: oil changes, die changes, parts inspections, and scheduling. I have a great sense of ownership and of accomplishment."[9]

STEP 3: Expect workers to make their own decisions, and to be accountable for them. There is no room for error when building jet engines; one misplaced rivet or undertorqued nut can lead to catastrophic failure. Workers at General Electric's (GE) aircraft-engine assembly facility in Durham, North Carolina, are expected to make their own decisions, and they take very personal responsibility for ensuring that the jobs they do are executed perfectly. The employees are organized into nine teams, with each team responsible for manufacturing a single engine, from beginning to end. Every time one of the engine's ten thousand parts is installed, each worker involved takes personal and public responsibility by entering his or her initials into a computer terminal that tracks the progress of the engine through the manufacturing process. The result? Seventy-five percent of the engines are perfect on delivery (most of the remaining 25 percent have only a single minor defect such as a paint scratch) and production costs at the team-based Durham plant are 12 to 13 percent less per unit than at GE's non-team-based engine plant outside Cincinnati, Ohio.[10]

STEP 4: Instill pride in the job and in the organization. At Jacksonville, Florida's Physician Sales and Service (PSS), a hundred-point checklist dubbed the Blue Ribbon book helps the company instill pride in its employees. Instead of spelling out *how* employees are supposed to get their jobs done, or listing everything that employees are not allowed to do, the Blue Ribbon book provides employees in PSS's fifty branch offices minimum guidelines for different aspects of the business. Twice a year, each branch undergoes surprise inspection by PSS's CEO or another member of the company's top-management team. Carrying the Blue Ribbon book in one hand, and checking off "yes" or "no" next to each of the hundred points, the executives produce a rating of each branch in fairly short order. No branch is punished for a poor score, and no one is fired or disciplined if a branch isn't up to par, but every branch wants to be the best at Blue Ribbon time. A high score is widely recognized, and the inspections are a source of bragging rights within the organization, fueling employees' pride in their work.[11]

STEP 5: Reward employees who take responsibility for product and quality. With more than $4 billion in annual sales, Nucor Corporation of Charlotte, North Carolina, ranks as one of the nation's largest steel makers. Nucor considers employee empowerment and responsibility for performance as hallmarks of their organization, and the company offers a variety of rewards for employees who meet or exceed their goals. In addition to giving employees generous across-the-board bonuses when company performance is unusually high, Nucor designed four incentive compensation plans to ensure that all employees have the opportunity to earn rewards and recognition for taking initiative and exceeding responsibilities:

- Production Incentive Plan: weekly bonuses, which average 80 to 150 percent of employee base pay, based on the productivity of operations and maintenance workers and their supervisors. Bonuses are not paid if equipment is not operating.
- Department Manager Incentive Plan: annual bonuses based on a calculation of the net income generated by each department manager, as a percentage return on assets. These bonuses typically average up to 80 percent of manager base pay.

- Professional and Clerical Bonus Plan: employees not covered by the previous two plans are eligible for bonuses based on their department's net income return on assets.
- Senior Officers Incentive Plan: top managers receive bonuses, paid in cash and stock, based on the company's net income as a percentage of shareholders' equity for the year.[12]

Potential Traps and Landmines

- **Managers who take all the credit, and give all the blame.** Employee responsibility is impossible in a team where the manager takes credit when things go well and places the blame squarely on employees when things go bad. An environment that values casting blame for failure more than finding solutions to nagging problems will likely produce more of the former than the latter. Punishing workers who take risks or come up with innovative ideas is a sure way to shut down employee engagement. It takes a team of employees working *together* to make great things happen; shine the spotlight on their efforts, successes, and accomplishments. The better *they* look, the better *you'll* look.
- **Managers, systems, and processes that don't hold employees accountable for their actions, whether good or bad.** Companies that fail to hold employees accountable for their actions invite mediocrity—or worse. However, during the past decade, employee accountability receded as a priority, as many companies grew fearful of alienating increasingly sensitive (and litigious) workers and eager to be more accommodating and less demanding in a competitive labor market. Companies cannot inspire excellence or earn loyalty if they do not require accountability. Hold employees accountable for their actions—both good and bad—and encourage them to hold themselves accountable as well.
- **Employees who avoid taking chances to improve products and services.** Today's business environment is not kind to complacency. Customer needs are constantly changing, and expectations are relentlessly growing.

The most successful organizations *anticipate* what their customers will require at some point in the future and meet them there, *ahead* of the competition. All this change requires employees who are willing to take chances and innovate to improve an organization's products and services. Instead of rewarding risk avoidance, reward employees who take initiative for moving the organization beyond the status quo, and encourage them to take on even more responsibility.

While some employees are naturally prepared to take responsibility and welcome the opportunity to do so, others may need encouragement from their peers and support from their managers. Praising positive performance, and helping workers correct their performance when outcomes are not up to par, set the stage for an empowered workplace where employees meet and exceed their responsibilities, whatever they may be.

4

Create Clarity of Roles

True freedom is not the absence of structure—letting the employees go off and do whatever they want—but rather a clear structure that enables people to work within established boundaries in an autonomous and creative way.

—ERICH FROMM, PSYCHOLOGIST, PHILOSOPHER, AND WRITER

Why does a company go through the trouble of hiring people to work for it, and spend vast amounts of money on salary, benefits, and training every year? The answer is obvious: to perform specific tasks and fulfill specific roles that it considers essential to its present operations, growth potential, or perhaps even its continued existence.

What tasks go with which roles? Once again, the answer is obvious . . . *sometimes*. If a business needs someone to accomplish the task of selling its products, it hires a salesperson, whose primary task will be to sell, not to service the computer network or to audit financial statements. However, in the current fast-paced, multitasked business environment the answer is often less readily apparent. In many companies, recent trends toward flat management and self-managed teamwork have undermined traditional clarity concerning the relationship between roles and tasks. In Orpheus, we have learned over the years that without clear role definition, workplace democracy can lead to orphaned responsibilities, duplication of effort, and processes that are inefficient at best and chaotic at worst. The lesson is clear: To remain effective and competitive, companies have no choice but to create clear roles for their employees.

Clear role definition is a necessary precondition for worker autonomy in any organization. Knowledge workers, in particular, thrive when they understand their roles in a broad context; the resulting autonomy makes them much more likely to find ways to contribute to their organization than employees operating in a command-and-control environment. Clear roles also allow employees to anticipate the ways that others within the organization will act, improving efficiency, creating easy lines of communication, and enhancing their ability to be responsive to changes in the business environment.

In Orpheus, clear role definition creates a stable and secure work environment that encourages each one of us to think creatively and liberates positive energy throughout the organization. Far from constraining employee flexibility and responsiveness, in our experience clear roles free people to grow into new areas of interest and competence, receive recognition for developing skills, and assume a reasonable degree of personal responsibility. Clear roles are essential for the success of Orpheus, as they are for any organization striving to improve quality and efficiency, while empowering its workers.

THE PRINCIPLE

Creating clarity of roles means ensuring that every member of an organization understands his or her roles and responsibilities, as well as the roles and responsibilities of his or her coworkers.

To remain competitive, today's companies are heavily dependent on their ability to adapt comfortably to rapidly changing market conditions. Yet, flexible organizations without clearly defined employee roles unavoidably find themselves diverting resources from productive tasks to coordinating departments and individuals.

Far too many companies fail to define employee roles clearly, or they allow once-clear role definitions to become ambiguous over time. Any organization that fails to address this situation risks a workforce cast adrift. While some employees with inadequately defined jobs react constructively by trying to seek (or create) clarity, many simply divest, grow cynical, or become indifferent to the value of their job functions to the company. Organizations that create clarity of roles for their employees can expect:

- Increased levels of employee responsibility and accountability for projects, goals, and deadlines
- Greater efficiency and increased worker productivity, as a result of decreased duplication of effort
- Improved morale, resulting from decreased internal ambiguity
- Increased satisfaction and loyalty, coupled with reduced rates of employee turnover

The most effective way to ensure that roles are clear and unambiguous is to put them in writing and review them with members of the organization. It is vitally important that these roles correspond to current organizational needs; consequently, definitions should be reviewed periodically and adapted as needed.

ORPHEUS: UNAMBIGUOUS ROLES AND RESPONSIBILITIES

It may seem paradoxical that a conductorless orchestra is grounded in crisp decision-making rules and lines of authority, but Orpheus's team-oriented model of collaboration presents its own set of challenges. Traditional orchestras certainly have clear enough roles, which have remained essentially unchanged for the past two centuries. Conductors control every aspect of music making, management decides when and where performances take place, and instrumentalists play music when, where, and how they are told.

We operate very differently, of course. From day one, by eliminating the conductor and empowering the musicians, Orpheus completely upended the established orchestral hierarchy. Once they jettisoned the traditional roles, our musicians were immediately faced with the urgent need to define new ones—clearly, carefully, and comprehensively.

For nearly thirty years, clear role definitions have brought order out of the very real potential for chaos that would otherwise be inherent in our multi-leader structure. Like most organizations, we are constantly striving to accomplish difficult goals, on time and within budget; naturally, our success depends on the ability of our members to work together effectively and efficiently to achieve them. To enhance this ability, we continually assess our organization's needs to establish exceptionally clear definitions, descriptions, and assignments for each of the hundreds of tasks that make up every Orpheus project. As a result, each member of each project team has a very well defined role and clear responsibilities to the group, to customers, and to themselves.

The Designated Leader

Even the pure democracy of chamber music, which Orpheus takes as its ideal, recognizes the special leadership role of the concertmaster with the Latin phrase *primes inter pares*, "first among equals." (The phrase refers to the first violin in a string quartet and, although these groups are models of collaboration and equality, the concertmaster has special duties and responsibilities.)

In our orchestra, the concertmaster is usually the designated leader of the entire group during rehearsals and performances. Every one of our members recognizes and works together to support the concertmaster's role, because our structure requires an effective concertmaster in order to function successfully.

In rehearsals, the concertmaster's primary role is to guide the orchestra through a collaborative process, bringing focus and shape to the musical interpretation, while encouraging others to contribute ideas to the discussion. When it's time to perform, only one person, generally the concertmaster, is responsible for cueing the orchestra to start. However, when the musical structure gives another instrumental section primacy, we designate someone other than the concertmaster to take on this leadership role. In other words, we use the characteristics and specifications of the product to decide who will be the designated leader for each moment of each performance. Regardless of who is chosen, the person selected to cue the orchestra is designated with that absolute and precise role and, when the moment arrives, every eye in the group goes in that direction automatically.

The Role of the Core

Every piece of music we perform has a leadership team of five to ten musicians to develop interpretive ideas and manage the rehearsal process. The role of these teams, which we call "cores," is to provide an operating framework of research, idea development, and leadership to the full orchestra.

Core members are selected for their leadership roles entirely by their colleagues. A special committee of orchestra members chooses the concertmasters—who function as de facto team leaders—for each piece we perform. Various instrumental sections (e.g., viola, oboe, French horn), in consultation with other orchestra members, then select players to be their representatives, assuring that a broad range of ideas and expertise will be built into the core process. In all cases, the members of a core group are selected based on judgments made by their peers about their professional strengths, insights into the challenges of specific pieces of music, and leadership styles. Our approach matches individual expertise to a clear, but shifting, set of roles, helping us to fully engage the organization's collective knowledge to develop superior musical products.

During the years before the musicians invented the core system, our rehearsals resembled free-for-alls, with each musician attending every rehearsal, and contributing ideas that were endlessly discussed and debated with colleagues. As a result, we needed fifteen or more full rehearsals to prepare for each concert, far more than the two to four typically required by conductor-led orchestras. By the late 1970s, rehearsals threatened to crowd out the numerous performance opportunities that were beginning to come our way, and it grew increasingly difficult for our members to have a meaningful impact on the product in the midst of such chaos. The system was too costly, inefficient, and frustrating to sustain itself.

In an effort to solve these problems, Orpheus introduced the core system, and it quickly improved rehearsal productivity and efficiency, while maintaining (and even enhancing) our collaborative approach to decision making. Today, it is a centerpiece of the Orpheus Process.

J. Richard Hackman, Cahners-Rabb Professor of Social and Organizational Psychology at Harvard University and a long-term observer of the dynamics of leadership in Orpheus, considers the role of the core to be a vital element in the success of Orpheus. Notes Hackman, "The details of the procedures that Orpheus uses might not work for a one-hundred-person orchestra. But, on the other hand, they didn't work for them either in their very early years. They had to come up with—in fact, actually invent—the concept of the core, which is a way of getting some involvement in the making of music that is reasonably efficient. And then, of course, the members of the core who are there while they are working through the interpretation and the artistic vision of the piece are in a position to bring the rest of the orchestra on board."

Everyone in Orpheus understands and respects that the core's role sometimes requires it to make decisions on behalf of the entire group. Says board chairman Gonzalo de Las Heras, "Without ever making it explicit, the dynamic of the group has made it quite clear that the core musicians for each piece have decision-making powers. Orpheus is not a direct democracy. Everyone can speak up, but the core group is clearly identified and is ultimately accountable to the entire orchestra for the success or the failure of that piece."

But unlike a conductor, who in a traditional orchestra has complete decision-making authority over music interpretation and rehearsal management, the core must lead by persuasion. Like every leader or leadership team in our organization, each core group must be able to take input, absorb criticism, and synthesize it to build consensus.

Clarity of Functions

Like so much else in our organization, clarity of roles starts with individuals giving absolute priority to their primary contribution toward our collective effort to produce the best possible musical product. A violinist is first and foremost a violinist, not a tour organizer or an accountant. Although we value suggestions and ideas from our violinists (and our tour organizers and accountants) about everything that goes on at Orpheus, it is clear to everyone that the violinist's job is, above all, to play violin.

We have learned from experience that in order to give employees the latitude to take on new responsibilities, while maintaining the quality of our products and efficiency of our operations, everyone in our organization must understand what roles exist, precisely who is in which role at any given moment, and by what criteria each individual's performance will be judged. There should never be confusion about formal employee roles within any organization, and we work hard to ensure that every person understands what he or she is expected to accomplish. In most cases, staff jobs and tasks are spelled out in written position descriptions or job specifications that are posted on the Orpheus Intranet, where they are readily available to everyone within the organization.

Board chairman Las Heras believes that clarity of roles is an essential element in the excellence of Orpheus's musical products, because it allows each member to know who is responsible for each individual decision. "Orpheus constantly delegates or expands decision making, but attributes it very clearly. That is very important, because when decision making is only diffused, it doesn't work. To be accountable for your decisions, you must first be identifiable. In Orpheus, if you make a mistake, you have to own up to it."

Clarity of roles is important to those inside our organization, but it's equally important to those who interface with us from the outside. Every day, we deal with customers, vendors, and business partners from all over the world. Since people tend to relate to organizations in standardized and fairly predictable ways, we need a clear and comprehensible distribution of roles and responsibilities; in other words, there have to be people within Orpheus who function in standardized industry roles. Without a high degree of clarity about how those roles are allocated internally, we could not function in the real world.

Musical Chairs

Decision-making assignments shift rapidly in response to our changing needs, and we draw great strength from the ability of our members to fulfill multiple and shifting management roles. Over the years, we have developed a unique and flexible structure that allows us to take full advantage of the extraordinary reservoir of talent within our organization. In Orpheus, a cellist may simultaneously be a trustee, and a violinist a regular presenter at management seminars; the concertmaster for the first piece in a performance often sits in the last row of the second violin section later that same evening. Several times I have stepped outside my primary role as executive director to design lighting for performances of contemporary music, utilizing my specialized skills in theatrical production.

In addition, we encourage everyone in the organization to identify and pursue special projects that directly engage their skills and interests. Many members have taken the initiative to involve composers or guest artists in collaborations with the orchestra; others have played an important role in designing new educational programs. These members typically maintain some kind of ongoing relationship with these projects, often functioning as a liaison with external partners and as a designated leader during rehearsals.

We also encourage our members to fulfill shifting roles on an informal basis when it will best serve our product and quality. For example, when the musicians much reach final decisions about interpretation, it is the concertmaster's role to guide the process and, acting on behalf of an existing consensus, articulate the outcome. But no matter how passionately the concertmaster (or any other musician) may advocate a point of view, insight and information are valued qualities in Orpheus, and any person or group with special knowledge or unusually clear perspective automatically has a clear and respected role to play in decision making.

Rules of the Game

In addition to having clear roles, we have rules that enhance our ability to operate in a flexible and team-oriented way, without compromising our focus on accomplishing our goals in an orderly, peaceful, and timely way. In any organization that operates through collaborative management, rules can decrease confusion and prevent (or resolve) disputes, but to be effective they must be widely understood, broadly respected, and consistent with the group's values, norms, and culture. In our case, rules balance all of our specialized and managerial roles against each individual's more general responsibility for the quality of our products, to ensure that the final result of the Orpheus Process is musical excellence.

Among our most important rules are the ones that we use to determine when individual members have decision-making authority and when a broader consensus is required. In Orpheus, decisions that have only limited impact on the group as a whole are typically left in the hands of the individuals fulfilling leadership roles that carry these specific responsibilities; they are expected to reach out to colleagues to resolve disputes or problems. Issues with broader implications become the focus of open discussion; in those cases, individuals occupying leadership roles tend to function as moderators and facilitators, reaching out to involve everyone in the group. Occasionally, the ultimate resolution of these broader issues—particularly if consensus can't be reached—is a vote. The vote is the final authority and, although it's not used very often, it's available when necessary.

Our primary business is live performance, which often requires us to make decisions in the moment. By ensuring that every individual in Orpheus recognizes the lines of decision-making authority that apply to each piece, concert, and job, these rules allow us to act quickly as well as collaboratively. For instance, when necessary the concertmaster, as the primary leader for cueing the orchestra during the performance, can often directly resolve matters with a personal choice during the concert.

As we'll see in chapter 7, this level of clarity fosters direct and productive conversations among orchestra members as well as between the administrative team and musicians, allowing all of us to work together effectively to achieve our goals. Clearly defined roles function as an organizational safety net that gives us the security we need to grant each individual the freedom to take initiative and make Orpheus successful.

Troubleshooting Roles

If roles aren't functioning effectively, what kinds of conclusions can be drawn, and what can be done about it? Although it's easy to blame the person in the responsible position (and sometimes that assessment has merit), sometimes it is useful to go deeper and ask questions, such as: Is the job designed in a way that is consistent with the organization, its structures, and its goals? Is it actually possible to fulfill the job's duties and responsibilities?

In Orpheus, we periodically evaluate the performance of our leadership structures, as well as the performance of our employees. For example, in 1998 a special committee of musicians, managers, and trustees recommended that we add the three "artistic director" positions to the administrative team, to be filled by members of the orchestra. The creation of these new roles (which will be discussed in detail in chapter 5) dramatically improved our internal communications and solved many long-standing problems in Orpheus. Nevertheless, two years later a second working group brought further clarity to the artistic director roles by refining their job descriptions, compensation structure, and performance criteria in light of our initial experiences. In addition, orchestra members evaluate the performance of the people they assign to the artistic director positions, making their decisions by voting colleagues in or out of these positions.

Over the years, we have discovered that by periodically reviewing and redesigning job descriptions, we are able to give everyone in the organization input into the design and definition of their jobs, with great benefit to our performance.

THE RITZ-CARLTON HOTEL COMPANY: DEPENDABILITY AND FLEXIBILITY

During the 1990s, an international revolution in customer service swept the business world. Where once it had seemed that customers and their needs were far down the list of priorities for many companies, suddenly companies put customers on top, encouraging employees to step out of their formal roles and duties to solve customer problems and to anticipate their needs. This pressure to put flexibility before clarity of roles, however, threatened businesses with a loss of employee accountability, and employees with decreased morale. To succeed, companies must find a balance between flexibility and clarity of roles, and they must communicate the importance of both to their employees.

The Ritz-Carlton Hotel Company, a $1.4 billion independently operated division of Marriott headquartered in Atlanta, Georgia, is widely considered to be one of the top hotel companies in the world. Ritz-Carlton's more than 21,800 employees working in thirty-nine luxury hotels and resorts around the world are given clear responsibility for and authority to achieve the company's goal of complete customer satisfaction. The company is evidently meeting its goal: in addition to receiving top marks from both leisure and business travelers, Ritz-Carlton was named the overall Best Practice Champion in the lodging industry in a comprehensive 1999 study by the Cornell School of Hotel Administration and has twice earned the coveted Malcolm Baldrige National Quality Award, first in 1992, at the beginning of the customer service revolution, and most recently in 1999. It is not only the first and only hotel company to win the Baldrige award, but it is also the first and only service company to win the award twice.

Clear and Flexible Roles

By its nature, the large hotel industry depends on the repeated execution of specific tasks at a high volume, and consequently employee roles are often very narrowly defined. A doorman's job is to assist guests in and out of the hotel, call for taxicabs, and perhaps summon a bellperson when necessary. A director of quality's job is to analyze data, facilitate teams, and direct measurable improvement in external and internal customer satisfaction. An assistant director of finance's job is to prepare financial statements, journal entries, and accruals, while managing the hotel's accounting department. Indeed, for decades many hotel staffs worked with such intense specialization that their ability to solve customer problems was hampered.

In response, beginning in the mid-1980s Ritz-Carlton decided to redefine employee responsibility in two ways.

First, employees continue to have clearly defined, specialized duties and projects; however, at Ritz-Carlton, individual responsibilities are tied to thirty processes that the hotel considers key to producing the best service in the industry. The company's detailed job descriptions, its quality improvement handbook (the GreenBook), and an annual thirty-day training certification process ensure that employees understand not just the tasks they are expected to perform during the course of a day, but the way in which their work affects other departments. Furthermore, each staff position at the company's hotels is assigned a "Talent+" profile that identifies clear criteria for excellent employee performance in his or her job.[1]

Second, Ritz-Carlton gives every employee the role of responding to specific customer needs and solving their problems as they arise. Before information technology gave organizations the ability to catalog a vast universe of possible customer needs and problems, the company created the Ritz-Carlton Credo, a statement of values that encourages employee innovation and creativity in meeting customer needs while fulfilling their assigned duties. The secret to Ritz-Carlton's success is its ability to instill clear employee roles and personal accountability while being responsive to specific customer expectations and problems. According to Theo Gilbert-Jamison, Ritz-Carlton's vice president of training and development, "Employees have clear roles. They understand, 'This is what my job is.' At the same time, they have the flexibility to break away to take care of guests and to take care of another employee. . . . We never want to lose a customer, so what we try to do if we do make a mistake is to instantly fix the problem. That is the responsibility of every employee. We say, 'If you receive a guest complaint, you own it.' You don't give it to someone else; you take care of it." All employees are cross-trained to help out in other departments, and the annual recertification requirement ensures that all employees are familiar with Ritz-Carlton's latest procedures.

Responding Efficiently

In the early to mid-1990s, Ritz-Carlton implemented a comprehensive process that gave managers and employees stronger guidelines for balancing specialized tasks and broader responsibility for customer service that, in keeping with the Ritz-Carlton credo, "enlivens the senses, instills well-being, and fulfills even the unexpressed wishes and needs of our guests." Among an employee's most important duties is tracking customer preferences and responses to service requests in the company's global CLASS database, which gives hotel staff around the world access to the likes and dislikes of more than 240,000 frequent Ritz-Carlton guests, and information about more than 1 million visitors and events.

In addition, employees must track several service quality indicators (SQI)—such as unresolved customer difficulties and abandoned reservation calls—each day as they fulfill their primary job responsibilities and customer needs. The SQI cover the twelve most serious service problems, weighted by a point value based on impact on customer satisfaction, that can occur in a hotel's daily operations, and they help employees empirically determine whether their specific or general job responsibilities take precedence in a situation.[2] The daily point value (the total number of occurrences for each problem multiplied by its assigned weight) for the hotel is disseminated every day to all employees, giving a measure of the team's overall customer service performance.

By putting "the genuine care of and comfort of our guests" as the company's highest goal, Ritz-Carlton has fashioned a strong, team-oriented environment where lateral service—employees helping other employees—is the norm, not the exception. Says Sean Garzee, senior door captain–Japanese Guest Relations for Ritz-Carlton, San Francisco, "It's the philosophy, the thought process, the ability to handle anything that comes your way instead of saying that, if it's not in your job title, you don't touch it." At the same time, employees are very well aware that they have a specific job to do, and that they are expected to perform it. Just because one customer has a problem doesn't, for example, justify inconveniencing five other customers who have to wait in line for an extra fifteen minutes while a well-meaning employee moves heaven and earth to find a solution.

Communicating Clarity of Roles

Making a rapid transition from performing one's assigned duties to stepping out of them to meet a customer need or solve a customer problem requires something extra of Ritz-Carlton employees to ensure that other customers are not inconvenienced and that employees don't respond to the same customer need as someone else. It also requires sophisticated systems for communication and role delegation.

When Ritz-Carlton employees step out of their primary job responsibilities to respond to a customer need or problem, they first notify those they work with—supervisors and/or coworkers—and ensure that someone can cover their basic job responsibilities in their absence. Only when they are assured that their primary duties will be covered do employees then step out of their formal job roles. They also consult the hotel's CLASS database to see how the customer's past problems may have been resolved or if another employee has already taken responsibility for solving the current difficulty.

Instilling clarity of roles for employees doesn't happen spontaneously; it takes a concerted effort throughout the organization to define multiple, and shifting, employee roles and then ensure that they are communicated, understood, and put into action consistently and at the highest levels of performance. According to Marguerite Dowd, administrative assistant to the sales and marketing directors at the Ritz-Carlton, Laguna Niguel, California, "Every job in the hotel, every position, has a clear definition of responsibilities, and they're clearly explained through your training."

The basic building block of communication within Ritz-Carlton is the daily lineup, a brief training session held at the beginning of each shift in each of the company's thirty-nine hotels worldwide. During the daily lineup, team leaders and employees communicate up and down the organization and laterally across all jobs. In addition to reporting news from the previous shifts and reviewing the hotel's scheduled events, leaders discuss what other hotel departments are doing. Says Dowd, "We're always well aware from our lineups what's going on in each department so that we can have a finger in the pie of everything else that goes on in the hotel." The hotel has identified more than two thousand potential service problems that could arise during a guest's stay or an event, and the daily lineup gives the staff an opportunity to determine who on the team will respond to the problems most likely to come up in the day's shift.

Every Worker Is a Knowledge Worker

Finally, according to Horst Schulze, Ritz-Carlton's president and chief operating officer, giving employees a role in planning their own work is a central factor in the company's ability to maintain high morale, reduce turnover, and attain higher performance levels. Therefore, employees are given broad discretion, including the authority to spend up to $2,000 to decide how to serve the hotel's customers. For example, when a guest couldn't find a particular silver chain that he wanted in the hotel's gift shop, Bella Conscentino, retail clerk at Ritz-Carlton, San Francisco, determined that performing her formal duties while upholding the values of the company meant briefly leaving the hotel premises to locate the item that the guest, a regular Ritz-Carlton customer according to the company's database, desired. After first notifying her manager to ensure that the gift shop was properly staffed, Conscentino left the hotel, bought the gift, and then personally delivered it to the grateful guest.

In another example, Steve Stagner, lead concierge for the Ritz-Carlton Club at Ritz-Carlton, San Francisco, knew that some guests were planning to make a trip to the Napa wine country, but had no hotel arrangements. Not satisfied with the possibility that his guests might be disappointed with their trip, Stagner drove to Napa and scouted out a number of possibilities for them, finding a hotel that was just right. The guests were so pleased with their experience that they booked an extra weekend's stay at the Ritz-Carlton when they returned from Napa.

Ritz-Carlton has become a popular model against which other organizations benchmark their own performance—so much so that courses offered by the Ritz-Carlton Leadership Center are in great demand from a variety of organizations. The Leadership Center was established in 1999 to provide Ritz-Carlton leaders with best-in-class training in the areas of professional business development, leadership, coaching, and mentoring, and many classes are taught by the company's senior leadership team. Since May 2000, more than twenty-five companies representing the financial, property management, automobile, manufacturing, medical, and restaurant industries have sent employees to the Ritz-Carlton Legendary Service or Leadership Orientation courses. These companies know that to compete successfully for employees, as well as customers, they need to adopt knowledge industry models like the ones employed by Ritz-Carlton and by Orpheus Chamber Orchestra.

Ritz-Carlton has found an approach that resonates with its workforce—employee satisfaction at the company is quite high; employee turnover decreased from 79 percent in 1989 to 30.2 percent in 1998. This compares quite favorably to the industry average of 52 percent.[3] Will these trends continue into the future? Only time will tell, but if loyal employees like Ritz-Carlton, Philadelphia, hostess Sylvie Galiazzi are any indication, then the answer is probably in the affirmative. Says Galiazzi, "I took a pay cut and left a management position to work here. I will retire at the Ritz-Carlton Hotel Company."[4]

PUTTING THIS PRINCIPLE INTO PRACTICE

Companies with unclear roles run significant risks—profound uncertainty and rampant confusion as employees attempt to figure out what their responsibilities are; disputes between workers unsure of the boundaries of their jobs; unnecessary frustration and duplication of effort; and critical tasks left undone. On the other hand, companies with clear roles are far more likely to have efficient and effective employees, working in concert to achieve a common set of objectives. Any organization attempting to clarify previously ambiguous roles must be prepared to invest time and commitment to develop and publicize formal, written job descriptions. Equally important, supervisors, managers and employees need the authority to evaluate positions as well as people on an ongoing basis, as new or temporary projects arise.

Five Steps for Creating Clear Roles and Direction

STEP 1: Develop written job descriptions. One of the surest and easiest ways to clarify roles, tasks, and duties within an organization is to put them into writing. A good model comes from the National Education Association (NEA), which has launched a national program to upgrade job descriptions for teachers. In addition to spelling out a precise list of duties, the NEA suggests that job descriptions answer the following questions:

- What is the purpose of this work?
- Why is this work important?
- What is accomplished by performing these tasks?
- How do we accomplish the performance of these tasks in order to provide a quality product?[5]

By answering these questions, employers can link employees' job descriptions to a sense of empowerment and responsibility for product and quality.

STEP 2: Clarify informal job responsibilities. Most employees have informal as well as formal responsibilities. For example, a payroll clerk may be expected to advise other employees regarding insurance claim procedures and participate in departmental quality-improvement efforts in addition to issuing paychecks, tracking employee leave, and data entry. Since these informal responsibilities are rarely included in a written job description, it's all the more important that they be clearly explained to employees by supervisors, so that each person understands the performance expectations that go with his or her position.

STEP 3: Constantly assess individual performance. One of the key responsibilities of any manager is periodically assessing the performance of his or her employees. Although many supervisors rely on annual performance reviews, there are significant benefits to more frequent assessments, since rapid identification and correction of emerging performance-related problems increase employee effectiveness and organizational productivity. The increasing popularity of teams complicates the efforts of companies to assess the performance of individual employees, since overall team performance can mask the deficiencies of particular members. Says James Bowers, vice president for chemistry industry consulting for the Hay Group, "Under the team reward structure, slackers enjoy the benefits of being on a team that succeeded despite them, not because of them. And so the challenge is to come up with measures for personal contributions that equate to effective teamwork." To help them identify what individual employees have done to make their teams more effective, supervisors and managers should consider including peer reviews in the assessment process.

STEP 4: **Publicize job responsibilities widely.** Organizations that treat job descriptions as classified information, to be filed away until the time of an employee's performance review, miss the point. Everyone needs to be clear about who is responsible for what within an organization, which requires widely distributing information about roles and making job descriptions accessible to all employees. This can be accomplished by placing job descriptions on a company Intranet or in a loose-leaf binder.

STEP 5: **Encourage employees to learn new roles and responsibilities (and then put them in writing).** Secretary Elaine Crawford of Sheboygan, Wisconsin–based sausage maker Johnsonville Foods came up with the idea of offering the company's products via mail order, and presented it to her boss. Instead of doing it himself, Crawford's boss assigned her to write up a business plan for the proposed operation. Johnsonville's management team approved the idea, and Crawford's boss put her in charge of the operation—formalizing her new role in the organization at the same time. The mail-order operation quickly became a success and a major source of revenue for Johnsonville.[6]

Potential Traps and Landmines

- **Job descriptions that are ambiguous, ignored, or don't exist at all.** There are no federal, state, or local laws that require organizations to maintain clear and understandable job descriptions, or any job descriptions at all. But if you've worked in an organization with poorly written, unclear, or ambiguous job descriptions, you might think that there ought to be. Fuzzy roles lead to fuzzy results. If people are unsure what their jobs are, chances are they aren't doing the tasks their companies need done, nor are they pursuing the goals that are most important to their employers. If your company doesn't have job descriptions, get them; if they already exist, make sure they are clear, comprehensible, and readily available to all employees at all times.

- **Excessive role overlap.** While some overlap between jobs can be helpful, too much can cause problems for employees and the organizations that employ them. When two people have jobs with excessively overlapping responsibilities, conflicts can arise as each employee tries to do the job his or her own way. Alternatively, each employee may believe that the other has taken responsibility for a particular job, resulting in work going undone. In both cases, the employees involved are likely to become frustrated; if projects are compromised, the entire organization may suffer. It's best to avoid role overlap as much as possible, but if you do decide to overlap employee roles, make certain that clear communication with and between the affected employees is frequent and ongoing.
- **Indefinite points of contact with customers and clients.** Today, more than ever, employees and customers need clear lines of communication, and customers should never be in the dark about who to contact when problems arise or questions need answers. Make sure your employees have clear titles that make sense to your customers, and be sure that everyone who deals with your company has easy access to a directory of all the people they'll ever need to contact.
- **Unrealistic expectations on the part of managers.** Many managers expect employees to know exactly what to do in every situation, but even the most talented and self-motivated employees need guidance from time to time, and all need proper training in their assigned responsibilities. Expect the best from your employees but don't expect the impossible, and don't expect them to read your mind. Give clear direction and offer your support and encouragement.

Clear roles are a valuable asset to any organization; they provide employees with a set of expectations for performance, as well as a framework for innovation and improvement. In Orpheus, clear roles are the foundation upon which we have built a flexible and collaborative process. They allow us to combine functions that cut across organizational boundaries and shift personnel from project to project, without confusion.

5

Share and Rotate Leadership

Go to the people
Learn from them
Love them
Start with what they know
Build on what they have
But of the best leaders
When their task is accomplished
Their work is done
The people will remark:
"We have done it ourselves."

–LAO-TZU

In a groundbreaking 1996 study that explored feelings and attitudes among people working in various job groups, Harvard professor Richard Hackman discovered that orchestral musicians ranked just below federal prison guards in job satisfaction.[1]

On the surface, this was a surprising conclusion. After all, professional orchestra musicians earn good salaries doing work they love to do, while spending their time traveling to glamorous places and basking in the applause of appreciative audiences the world over. But Hackman's research revealed sharp contradictions between the intensely creative and self-directed inner worlds inhabited by musicians and the rigid and static hierarchies that dominate the working environments of virtually all symphony orchestras. Two of the findings were particularly revealing—musicians outranked all other job categories in the strength of their internal motivation, but they were in the bottom third when asked about their satisfaction with opportunities for career growth.[2] Clearly, the clash between the forces that motivate musicians and the organizational structures that confine them to fixed, subservient roles has a great deal to do with the widespread frustration and job dissatisfaction found among orchestral musicians.

Perhaps not surprisingly, knowledge workers in many fields are motivated by essentially the same attributes. Like musicians, most knowledge workers pursue careers that allow them to perform work that they love and value the opportunity to experience creative engagement in their work through self-expression and problem solving.

Since knowledge workers are the most highly productive and value-adding employees in today's information-based economy, most organizations can reap enormous benefits by cultivating congenial work environments that reenforce these workers' naturally occurring internal motivation and by fostering their opportunities for self-direction, variety, and professional growth.

But all too often, knowledge workers are held back (or turned off) by organizational structures that deny them the ability to contribute freely and creatively to their companies' products, services, or solutions. When educated, creative, talented, motivated, and experienced employees are consistently locked out of meaningful leadership roles—whether goal setting, decision making, prioritizing, or performance evaluation—the entire organization suffers. Conversely, sharing and rotating leadership fuels employee motivation, leading to improved productivity and organizational effectiveness.

THE PRINCIPLE

Research by Carnegie Mellon business professor Robert Kelley has revealed widespread dissatisfaction with corporate leadership among employees. Forty percent of those surveyed believed that their bosses had questionable leadership abilities, and almost as many believed that their bosses had "ego problems" that made them feel threatened by and defensive around talented subordinates and new ideas. Less than half of all leaders inspired trust in their subordinates, and only one in seven was seen as a potential role model to emulate.[3] When such shortcomings (or the perception of them) pervade a company, even otherwise credible leaders are undermined and followers feel cast adrift.

Apparently, there are two principal downsides to the traditional model of fixed organizational leadership. Not only does the failure to take full advantage of the skills and talents of every worker represent a high opportunity cost borne by the entire company, but disenfranchised employees also tend to grow cynical about the elite few who comprise a leadership nucleus. As a result, organizations that restrict leadership to a small number of people tend to suffer poor morale, high turnover, and the loss of competitive advantage.

Knowledge workers seek challenge, stimulation, and variety, and organizations can provide a motivational work environment by actively encouraging employees to rotate in and out of positions of leadership on the projects and tasks that most interest them, regardless of their rank or position. Rather than restricting leadership opportunities, smart companies call upon multiple ideas and quickly mobilize their entire organizations to solve pressing problems by finding ways to structure leadership responsibilities among several employees. Organizations that share and rotate leadership can expect the following benefits:

- The emergence of more leaders from employee ranks

- Higher levels of employee commitment resulting from increased feelings of ownership
- Increased diversity of ideas and approaches to capitalizing on opportunities and dealing with problems
- Increased employee excitement, energy, and engagement in their jobs

Organizations that motivate and engage the skills of all their employees by sharing and rotating leadership roles gain a significant competitive advantage in today's economy because their employees are happier and more productive and exhibit increased loyalty in the face of adversity. In the increasingly competitive global marketplace, even a small edge can make a significant difference in the prospects for a corporation's long-term success.

Orpheus: A Hierarchy of Equals

In Orpheus, we stand the traditional model of fixed organizational leadership on its head by sharing and rotating leadership among the members of the orchestra. We start by assuming that leaders and followers are equals, and every one of our members is able—and expected—to function in both roles. By empowering a large group of talented, self-confident musicians to take leadership roles and make decisions, our structure motivates each individual to actively contribute to the achievement of our goals and objectives. But, as we soon discovered, developing a unified approach to product development and a strategic approach to business decision making are especially challenging when leadership roles are shared and rotated.

The Effective Orpheus Leader

To successfully meet these challenges, we devote ourselves to identifying and cultivating the four principal qualities that we consider essential to effective leadership in Orpheus:

1. **Balance.** Our leaders must constantly shift between advancing a point of view and soliciting ideas and information from others. Knowing when and how to balance advocacy and facilitation, individual perspective, and group process is critical.
2. **Fairness.** Openness to the ideas of others and willingness to suspend disbelief while trying them out are critical components of the ability to serve as an honest broker. Our leaders must earn the confidence of the group by creating a working atmosphere of fairness and credibility.
3. **Synthesis.** All successful leaders in Orpheus routinely incorporate the ideas of others into their own personal strategies. We constantly rely on designated leaders to build consensus by synthesizing the group's best ideas and approaches into a coherent whole.
4. **Decisiveness.** The ability to make decisions when needed and to lead through action in performance are essential in any organization. Our entire process can quickly unravel if our leaders lack these skills, and we place a very high premium on energetic, decisive, and—when necessary—commanding leadership.

Diverse Leadership

The core system is a unique innovation that brings coherence and efficiency to our decision-making process, while allowing us to share and rotate leadership among the entire membership of the orchestra over the course of a season. In a typical concert with four or five different pieces of music on the program, twenty or more musicians will take on leadership roles at some point in the evening.

Core groups have four distinct and important functions in the Orpheus Process:

First, the core group is charged with the responsibility of choreographing shifting leadership roles as defined (or implied) by the musical score. In effect, this choreography gives the entire orchestra a highly flexible team structure that is custom-designed to the demands and specifications of each piece of music we perform, allowing us to work on each piece as if it were chamber music.

Second, the core group develops an initial interpretive concept for each piece of music, much as a commercial organization might use a product-development team to create prototypes. This function includes research into the history, style, and structure of the music; development, such as discovering challenges and details in the music that may not be evident in a larger group of thirty or forty people; product design, including preliminary choices concerning musical interpretation; and communication to the orchestra as a whole. Though the core group's concept is crucial to setting the stage for ultimate decisions of the full orchestra, it isn't the final word. Says violinist Ronnie Bauch, "These core groups formulate one interpretation of a piece. It's not necessarily *the* interpretation. Sometimes it's just a starting point."

Third, the core group shapes the full orchestra's rehearsal process, deciding what movements will be rehearsed first, and for how long. Rehearsal time is expensive and limited; musicians have to be paid and space has to be rented. The core group, working with another musician-leader, the rehearsal coordinator, helps ensure that our rehearsals balance efficiency with openness—the opportunity for each musician to fully participate in shaping the final product. This function corresponds to a classic function of leadership in any organization—the core establishes priorities and allocates resources in the most effective way.

Fourth, the core provides direct leadership in performance, holding the group together and making on-the-scene decisions for the entire orchestra when delay would be disastrous, and it is impossible to draw on everyone's expertise.

Our cores act in much the same way as a project team or self-managing work team in a business environment to focus the efforts of a small group of people intently around a common objective and a common problem. The core system is a particularly powerful management tool within Orpheus because cores provide interdisciplinary leadership for naturally existing teams within the orchestra (individual sections such as violas and clarinets, larger groupings such as strings and woodwinds). There's no one looking over the group's shoulder, no right and no wrong, and there's an unbounded freedom to create and innovate.

Three Stages of Leadership

Although each full Orpheus rehearsal is a unique encounter between a leadership team and the larger group with its own individual shape and dynamic, we have developed an effective three-step sequence of information sharing, exploration, and decision making that our leaders rely on to shape the final product.

In the first step, leaders demonstrate their essential insights into the music through action, by leading the full orchestra in a read-through of the entire piece. The group's role is to do its best to follow the core's directions, in effect trying these ideas "on for size." The read-through is often preceded by discussion and is typically followed up by repetition—all intended to clarify the group's understanding of their leaders' intentions. In business, this step correlates to presentations made by team leaders, explaining the background behind particular opportunities or problems, and outlining their proposed approaches and responses.

In the second step, everyone in the orchestra is encouraged to freely put forth ideas derived from his or her own preparatory work before the first rehearsal, including ones that differ sharply from the core's initial concept for the piece. As each member voices ideas, the entire group experiments with different aspects of musical interpretation while exploring alternative ways to distribute leadership roles during performance. Ultimately, the individuals designated to fulfill those roles provide critical input. This step is analogous to the brainstorming process that business teams often use to generate ideas during meetings. During a brainstorming session, criticism of ideas is temporarily withheld to encourage the widest possible variety of input. After enough ideas are on the table, the team winnows out all but the most promising.

In the third step, the core leads the full orchestra in decision making. Its role is subtle—to balance its own original concept with the orchestra's collaborative vision, thereby leading a process that results in the best possible musical product. Cores typically approach this task by attempting to build support from various constituencies within the orchestra. Approaches include:

- **Representative democracy.** Each member of the core is also a representative of an instrumental section in the orchestra; therefore, everyone in the larger group has some degree of ownership of the ideas advocated by someone on the leadership team. In the business world, representing all departments on teams makes them more effective.

- **Strategic alliances.** Often, the musical structure of a piece brings instrumental sections together to form a melody, rhythm, or harmony. Consensus among these musicians often proves decisive, even when the larger group becomes involved. Similarly, allowing all the departments involved in "back office" functions to identify a common objective makes a team's decision making more effective.

- **Working with opinion leaders.** For every piece we perform, informal, unofficial opinion leaders emerge. These are usually musicians with special experience or knowledge about particular historical periods, musical genres, or composers. Concertmasters and core members who work with opinion leaders in their advance preparation, incorporating their input into their vision, are far more likely to ultimately gain the orchestra's support and full energy. Every business has both formal and informal knowledge hierarchies, each wielding power and influence in the organization. Identifying and working with both is essential for leaders hoping to achieve their goals and have a lasting impact on any organization.

Recordings are a special test case for our system of shared and rotating leadership. For financial reasons, there is extreme pressure to efficiently use studio session time, meaning we have less time to search for consensus. Furthermore, the choices made by the group are not open for reconsideration, and the outcome is permanent. In the title piece of *Points of Departure*, an album of unusually complex and demanding twentieth-century music, our concertmaster met this challenge by working closely with two musicians who had extensive knowledge of contemporary music, even though neither one was on the core leadership team for that piece. With their input thoroughly integrated into the leadership approach, consensus was reached on many difficult issues, on time and within budget. The album ultimately became one of the orchestra's most critically acclaimed.

Because of the strong leadership skills our members have developed over the years, and careful consensus-building before and during rehearsals (an important characteristic of the Orpheus Process that will be discussed in chapter 8), it is extremely rare that we find ourselves deadlocked.

The Three Coordinators

As we have already seen, Orpheus divides the traditional rehearsal and performance roles of the conductor into leadership positions that are rotated and shared among the entire orchestra on a piece-by-piece basis. In most orchestras, the principal conductor also functions as the organization's monolithic artistic director. In contrast, we have developed a system that vests artistic direction collectively in a team of three coordinators, who are elected by the members of the orchestra and serve as part of our administrative team for set terms. Each of the three coordinators fulfills specific leadership roles that tackle the overarching central artistic plan of the organization in an efficient, team-based approach:

- The artistic coordinator serves as team leader and is responsible for artistic administration and the development of new ideas for programs and projects.

- The program coordinator develops repertoire ideas, including proposals of commissioning projects and collaborations with guest artists.
- The personnel coordinator works with the operations department to make sure that personnel decisions reflect and respond to the artistic needs of the orchestra.

Collectively, the team is known as the "artistic directors." It works with the rest of our administrative team to promote strong two-way communication between the orchestra and management, maintain and enhance our artistic quality, and strengthen our managerial choices and strategic decisions by facilitating the artistic input of the orchestra's members. Collaboration is close and constant.

Interactive Leadership

Within Orpheus, there is a constant flux and interplay between leaders and followers; individuals switch back and forth between leading and following many times during the course of a rehearsal as the orchestra tries out different approaches to playing a piece and shares feedback. We believe that the quality of these interactions allow us to provide our customers—the people who pay to attend our concerts and purchase our albums, and the concert producers, recording companies, and broadcasters that hire us to perform—with a superior product. They also contribute significantly to the uncommonly strong level of loyalty and commitment of our members, and our remarkably low turnover rate. (As mentioned in chapter 2, the average tenure for an Orpheus member is eighteen years.)

Bill Starbuck, ITT Professor of Creative Management at the Stern School of Business at New York University, uses classic 1950s-era studies of small-group decision making as an analytical tool to explore the strength of our system of sharing and rotating leadership. Says Starbuck, "A lot of organizations get into trouble because they are dependent on one leader who can't satisfy all of the group's needs. Orpheus has evolved a shared leadership that is more effective than having just one leader."

Starbuck breaks leadership functions into three areas—guiding accomplishments, morale and camaraderie: "There are some groups that have what the social psychologists call 'great men' leaders, meaning someone who is able to perform all these different roles. Orpheus splits the roles out into at least three different people—a task leader who knows how the music ought to be played and has studied the history of the performance of this piece and understands that side of it; an emotional leader who makes a joke at a time when there is a lot of tension and unhappiness; and a social leader who organizes the picnics and parties and whatever."

Teaching Others to Lead

Is there such a thing as a "born leader"? Researchers have grappled with the question for years, but the best answer seems to be "perhaps." Self-confidence, charisma, and intelligence all contribute to the image of leadership, and all are traits that some people seem to be born with, or at least acquire at a very early age. What is certain, however, is that leadership skills can be taught and learned, and that as talented individuals practice being leaders within an organization, they get better at it. Of course, when leaders get better at leading, the company, its employees, and its customers benefit.

In Orpheus, as in every corporation, certain people gravitate toward the leadership positions while others tend to shy away from them. But regardless of what roles our members ask to take on, everyone in our organization gets the opportunity and encouragement to lead, if he or she desires. We constantly strive to provide opportunities for everyone in the organization to develop new skills as they grow into new leadership roles.

Santa Clara, California–based computer chipmaker Intel develops its new leaders with a unique model program. At Intel, *every* leader in the company, from chairman Andrew Grove all the way down to the company's many first-line supervisors, must teach leadership as a part of his or her job. In fact, a portion of each supervisor's bonus is tied to whether or not he or she has actively participated in teaching others to lead.

Grove believes employees learn better from other employees, not from outsiders. In his book *High Output Management,* he asserts that "Training must be done by a person who represents a suitable role model. Proxies, no matter how well versed they might be in the subject matter, cannot assume that role. The person standing in front of the class should be seen as a believable, practicing authority on the subject taught."[4]

Intel publishes a catalog of classes taught by the company's leaders, covering subjects ranging from strategic planning to proper telephone etiquette to how to operate the extremely complex ion implanter, a device used in the manufacture of computer chips. Grove himself has taught classes on preparing and delivering performance reviews, conducting productive meetings, and the Intel Way.

By having experienced, on-site leaders teach their colleagues, Intel conveys its corporate culture from one generation to the next, and new leaders learn from the mistakes of those who have gone before them. Says one middle manager at Intel, "All of the guys that teach are busy, so, in some ways, they wish they didn't have to. But they know its important [that] managers that have 'been there' teach others."[5] Trainers brought in from outside a company can teach valuable skills and bring fresh perspective, but the best lessons are often taught by those with the benefit of having lived them.

W. L. GORE AND ASSOCIATES: SHARED LEADERSHIP IN MANUFACTURING

We've seen how the principle of shared and rotated leadership, where leaders emerge from the organization and take charge of projects as the need arises, works for the Orpheus Chamber Orchestra. But how does it work for a manufacturing business, particularly one in an industry where rigid hierarchies have been the norm for decades and even, for some companies, for centuries?

You may not have heard of W. L. Gore and Associates, Inc., of Newark, Delaware, but chances are you've heard of its products. You may even have used them. The manufacturer's most famous product, Gore-Tex, is the breathable, lightweight material that lets perspiration out while blocking wind and rain, and is widely used in a variety of outdoor clothing from skiing jackets to hiking boots to mountain-climbing pants. Gore's creative employees, called "associates," have developed an almost endless variety of other products out of PTFE (polytetrafluoroethylene), the amazingly versatile key ingredient in Gore-Tex: hernia repair patches, dental floss, space suits, surgical sutures, air filters, guitar strings, and more.

When former DuPont executive Bill Gore founded the company in 1958, he started with a clear vision for a workplace like no other, one that would unleash the creative powers of all its employees. At Gore, all employees (there are currently more than six thousand of them) serve on one large team. Instead of a traditional hierarchy of managers and workers with fixed titles and roles, Gore organized his company around a loose network of employees—a lattice organization—who are responsible to each other and to the company's many different projects.

The Lattice Organization

When Bill Gore labeled this new company structure a lattice organization, he was inspired by the unique orderly structure of atoms in a crystal. In Gore's words, "Every successful organization has an underground lattice. It's where news spreads like lightning, where people can go around the organization to get things done." A lattice organization has no formal hierarchy; titles, ranks, and layers of management do not exist, nor do bosses in the traditional sense of the word. At Gore, employees are "sponsors" and "associates."

The Gore lattice organization has the following six characteristics:

1. There are direct lines of communication—person to person—with no intermediary.
2. There is no fixed or assigned authority.
3. Sponsors, not bosses, guide employees.
4. Natural leadership also requires followership.
5. Objectives are set by those who must "make them happen."
6. Tasks and functions are organized through commitments.

Sponsors are not simply bosses with a trendy new label; they champion their associates and help them succeed within the organization. Sponsors act as guides, coaches, and mentors, rather than the traditional roles of task-master, overseer, or disciplinarian. Each job candidate must find a sponsor before he or she will be hired by the company; no sponsor, no job.

Approximately 20 percent of Gore employees sponsor staff, and every associate must have at least one sponsor. Sponsors gain no special benefits from their positions; there are no reserved parking spaces, special dining rooms, or corner offices. Strikingly, they hold no more organizationally vested authority than any other associate. Aside from a few titled positions such as president, secretary, and treasurer, all required by corporate law, Gore's organizational structure is completely and utterly flat.

But don't confuse the lack of hierarchy with a lack of leadership. W. L. Gore and Associates depends on leaders for their company's success, and leaders can be found throughout the organization. What makes Gore different from a traditional corporation is that leaders emerge from the company as the need arises, rather than from formal appointment by the company's management team. Leaders at Gore don't gain their power and authority because of their position on the organization chart, their job title, or the size of their paycheck; leaders at Gore gain power and authority by attracting followers, fellow associates who are willing to work toward the same goals as the leader.

Genesis of a New Project

Every new product or project starts when a Gore employee pursues an idea. But employees cannot chase every idea; sponsors and associates alike convince others to join them in realizing their vision before even the best ideas find their way into production. According to associate Terry Kelly, a business leader in the company's military-fabrics division, this isn't always an easy task. According to Kelly, "Although I'm a business leader for military fabric, I'm a leader only if there are people who are willing to follow me. A project doesn't move forward unless people buy into it. You cultivate followership by selling yourself, articulating your ideas, and developing a reputation for seeing things through."[6]

Kelly first identifies and resolves any potentially fatal flaws that could lead others to immediately shoot down her idea, no matter how good it might be. She says, "Let's say that I've come up with a design for a winter sleeping bag for the military. I'd go to the person responsible for marketing the bag and find out whether there's demand for it. If there isn't, I'd go back and try to reposition the plan. If he's excited by the idea and thinks it's viable, I'd bring him in on the project to help me develop it."

Next, Kelly pulls together a team of associates from across the company—including sales, design, and manufacturing—who believe strongly enough in the idea to develop it as a group. She gets them excited about the idea, and then allows the team to take it to the next level. "It's a process of giving away ownership of the idea to people who want to contribute and be a part of it," says Kelly. "The project won't go anywhere if you don't let people run with it."

Finally, Kelly shows her coworkers the contribution that her proposed product will make to the company's bottom line. This step cements her team's commitment to the project, and ultimately propels it forward. "People here understand that the growth of our business with the military is absolutely critical to our overall success," Kelly explains. "If I paint a convincing argument that we aren't giving the soldier our best product, then Gore employees need to think about that. And I have to show them that through their lack of action, they are opting out of the company's future."

W. L. Gore's unique concept of leadership works in the real world; the company continues to grow and prosper, with 1999 revenues of $1.45 billion placing Gore at 115 on the corresponding Forbes Private 500 ranking of privately held companies, up from 135 in 1998 and 157 in 1997. Gore has also become a model of a new kind of company, one that taps the leadership skills of all its employees and encourages them to make a real difference in Gore's culture and products.

It's no accident that W. L. Gore & Associates has been recognized as one of the "100 Best Companies to Work for in America" by *Fortune* magazine all five times the list has been published. Without the usual organization chart and formal titles, Gore's lattice structure unleashes the creativity of its employees by allowing them to champion new ideas and lead projects and people when they feel strongly enough about an idea, inspiring everyone in the company to follow their lead.

PUTTING THIS PRINCIPLE INTO PRACTICE

Finding methods for sharing and rotating leadership may be difficult. Old habits and fixed organizational hierarchies aren't easy to break, especially in companies where employees and managers have been conditioned to think that the key to success in every job is to follow the boss's orders.

However, as more and more businesses become information-based, using fewer employees to produce expanded results, organizations where everyone has the opportunity to lead will certainly be the most successful. Companies that can tap their employees' expertise, problem-solving skills, and self-direction enjoy a serious competitive advantage: motivated and satisfied workers who consistently hit company targets and meet unexpected challenges, even when formally appointed leaders are not available.

Five Steps for Expanding Your Leadership Circle

STEP 1: **Create a supportive environment.** Many companies, managers, and supervisors assert that they want their employees to take on leadership roles within their organizations, but then stop their employees when they try to do it. Be sure your workers know that they will get the support they need as long as their initiatives meet two criteria: the potential to benefit the company and forthright communication with designated supervisors about successes and setbacks. State this message loudly, clearly, and repeatedly. To get this message across to employees, Hershey Foods Corporation's (Hershey, Pennsylvania) chairman Richard Zimmerman created an award, the Exalted Order of the Extended Neck, for employees who take chances in their jobs for the benefit of the company. In Zimmerman's words, the purpose was to reward people who "were willing to buck the system, practice a little entrepreneurship, and stand the heat for an idea they really believe in."

STEP 2: **Train employees to lead, as well as to follow.** While some workers come to the job with extensive leadership experience, others need to be trained in basic leadership skills and techniques before they can become effective leaders. Offer leadership training to *all* employees, not just supervisors and managers, and pair workers with mentors who can demonstrate effective leadership skills. Followership—doing what needs to be done in an organization without having to be told to do it—is an equally important skill for employees to have. According to Carnegie Mellon business professor Robert Kelley, companies can build followership into their corporate culture by establishing orientation programs that stress the importance of exemplary followership, training programs that teach and hone followership skills, performance evaluation systems that rate how well individuals follow, and role modeling, wherein leaders demonstrate followership skills.[7]

STEP 3: **Encourage employee initiative.** Whether they know it or not, employees have the power to make a substantial positive impact on a company and its products; sometimes all it takes is the support of a boss who encourages employees to step into leadership positions. Managers should actively support and encourage employee initiative and the leadership behavior that goes along with it. Says Dean Spitzer, motivation expert and senior consultant for IBM Corporation, "I am convinced that the most successful organizations are the ones that actively encourage employees to take initiative, and the least successful ones are those that stifle initiative. Anyone can 'go through the motions,' but the behaviors that all organizations need in order to be successful require employee initiative. Creativity requires initiative. Outstanding customer service requires initiative. High quality requires initiative. In fact, virtually every organization was started by one or more people who took initiative to create a product, meet a need, serve a client, and organizations continue to thrive only if initiative continues."[8]

STEP 4: **Tear up your organization chart.** Potential leaders can be found anywhere in a company, not just behind doors marked with titles such as vice president, director, and project manager. Instead of allowing your organization chart to determine your company's leaders, allow your employees to decide for themselves and support them when they step into leadership roles. Self-managing teams of workers at the Saturn division of General Motors (Spring Hill, Tennessee) have taken on many of the roles and duties of traditional managers, taking responsibility for accounting, developing, and executing budgets, and hiring and firing their own members. In this wholesale reinvention of the standard manufacturing hierarchy, workers thrive on the chance to lead while experienced staff are freed from management functions and allowed to focus on their most value-adding skills.

STEP 5: **Reward leadership behavior.** In the words of management expert Tom Peters, "Well-constructed recognition settings provide the single most important opportunity to parade and reinforce the specific kinds of new behavior one hopes others will emulate."[9] If you want leaders to emerge throughout your corporation, then you've got to reward and recognize employees when they exhibit leadership behavior. This will reinforce the behavior of nascent leaders, and others will be encouraged to follow their example. Management at 3M (St. Paul, Minnesota) rewards employees who take the lead in developing and implementing new products by supporting them in setting up their own businesses within the company. If their businesses succeed, employees receive raises and promotions, and can spin the initiative out from 3M, which retains an ownership stake.

Potential Traps and Land Mines

- **Managers who talk a good story about giving workers leadership opportunities but who then punish employees who speak up or try something new.** Make it clear to all employees that you support leadership behavior that emerges from *any* part of your organization, and let your managers and supervisors know that you expect them to support, coach, and mentor workers who are ready, willing, and able to lead. Give your managers and supervisors the tools they need by training them in effective delegation techniques, and then reward managers and supervisors who learn to delegate effectively.
- **The process within the organization takes precedence over your work for clients, customers, vendors, suppliers, and others outside of the organization.** When all of your employees participate in leading your organization, there's going to be a buzz in the office, as newly engaged individuals turn to one another for expertise and guidance. But the most important dialogue should always be your employees' contacts with customers and everyone else you do business with. Build serving stakeholders and constituents into your definition of good leadership and consider employees' external relationships with customers, professional colleagues, and others as an essential part of developing their leadership skills.
- **A few individuals dominate leadership opportunities within an organization to the exclusion of other employees.** It's relatively easy for people who are ambitious or who exude confidence to hijack leadership roles unless your company plays close attention. Constantly bring new people into positions of leadership and ensure that these jobs don't default to the same people time after time. Train managers to understand that the advantage of sharing leadership is not only that skillful new leaders

emerge, but that sharing leadership also unleashes the creative energy of every member of the team.

- **Leaders who do not take responsibility for the impact of their decisions.** When you distribute leadership beyond a small group of professional managers you run the risk that newly empowered leaders will fail to accept or understand the responsibilities that go with their authority. Be clear that taking responsibility is an important leadership characteristic, and then create evaluation systems that take personal responsibility into account.

Sharing and rotating leadership encourages all employees to play active roles in making decisions for the organization's benefit. Whether in an orchestra or a corporation, this principle allows every person to have a voice in the kinds of products and services that will be developed and delivered to customers, how they will be delivered, and in what form. Ultimately, your happier, more creative and engaged employees will lead your company to better products and services and more satisfied customers and clients.

6

Foster Horizontal Teamwork

Soloists are inspiring in opera and perhaps even in small entrepreneurial ventures, but there is no place for them in large corporations.

—NORMAN R. AUGUSTINE,
FORMER PRESIDENT AND CEO,
LOCKHEED MARTIN

As the speed of competition in business increases, more and more companies are discovering that vertical organizational ladders can hinder their ability to respond quickly and strategically. Traditional formal hierarchies, relying on just a few top managers to communicate important information between parts of the company, no longer work very efficiently or effectively. The alternative? Teamwork that cuts across departmental boundaries.

By working together in "horizontal" teams, each individual knowledge worker can easily contribute a unique set of strengths to the development and implementation of intelligent solutions. In *The Wisdom of Teams,* Jon Katzenbach and Douglas Smith provide substantial evidence of the impressive track record of teamwork, from Honda Circles to 3M's action teams to Whole Foods's self-managing work groups. According to the authors' research, in nearly every industry teams "outperform individuals acting alone or in larger organizational groupings, especially when performance requires multiple skills, judgments, and experiences."[1] But, as management guru Peter Drucker points out, instituting real teamwork means encouraging everyone's ideas and treating all members of the team as equals, and companies need to organize and empower teams of employees in which no "knowledge ranks higher than another; each is judged by its contribution to the common task rather than by any inherent superiority or inferiority. . . . [T]he modern organization cannot be an organization of boss and subordinate."[2]

In a knowledge-based economy, compartmentalization and rigid hierarchy severely limit employee and organizational performance. On the other hand, horizontal teams, when deployed effectively, can foster a creative and dynamic environment that enhances productivity. According to Drucker, such teams allow each employee to leverage his or her expertise, leadership skills, and creativity to make informed decisions. In view of the benefits, it is surprising that so many businesses give short shrift to real teams and teamwork—saying (and thinking) they do it, but all too often renaming old work groups while maintaining the traditional chains of information and command.

Similarly, orchestras may appear to be model team-based organizations, composed of several instrumental groups working together, but just as in corporate America, teamwork rarely plays a significant role in their repertoire. Although different sections sometimes rehearse separately before the full group comes together, in conventionally structured orchestras these small rehearsals serve primarily to sharpen each musician's technical command and to harmonize details of execution rather than to generate ideas or make decisions. What's more, orchestral musicians rarely consider themselves to be part of a larger organizational team; their relationship to the administrative management, support staff, and volunteers is typically remote, and frequently estranged.

The opportunity cost to symphonic organizations is enormous. Says Albert K. Webster, formerly the managing director and executive vice president of the New York Philharmonic and currently a consultant to the Helen F.

Whitaker Fund, "I am convinced that the musicians of our orchestras are an undervalued, underutilized, and underappreciated resource of extraordinary potential with respect to nonartistic—administrative or managerial—matters."

In Orpheus, we use horizontal teams to take full advantage of our members' musical ideas and expertise. We also promote and rely heavily on musician involvement in all matters affecting the organization including governance issues, administration, management, and artistic decision making. We have found that the most effective vehicle for this involvement are teams of individual members and employees, each taking responsibility for working with colleagues in formal and informal groups, which look for opportunities and solve problems throughout the organization.

We believe that our members, like many knowledge workers, are quintessential problem solvers, and that Webster's observations about musicians have broad applicability to knowledge workers in many fields: "Many have wonderfully creative ideas: why can't we learn to truly listen to them? Many of them have talents and skills that rarely find expression within our institutions. A full partnership is not only possible, it is essential."[3]

THE PRINCIPLE

Fostering horizontal teamwork means encouraging employees to work together to solve problems and ensuring that teams have the authority to put their solutions into action. The bottom-line value of teams and teamwork in business has received a great deal of attention over the past decade, and many companies now recognize that well-functioning horizontal teams, pulled from diverse departments, lead to:

- Improved communication across traditional organizational lines
- Improved organizational ability to capitalize on opportunities
- Better solutions to difficult problems

- Improved quality and better customer service
- More empowered, engaged, and enthusiastic employees

For thirty years, Orpheus has met a wide range of product development and management needs by investing groups of employees with authority and responsibility. We have learned firsthand how to promote integrated and effective teamwork, relying almost entirely on ad hoc teams, which we use to marshal the skills and experience of many employees to address specific projects as needs arise.

Although it is widely recognized that individual employees can multiply their results by working together to achieve common goals, there has been relatively little focus on the steps organizations can take to build truly effective teams. In the sections that follow, you will see how Orpheus, the San Diego Zoo, and executive recruiting firm Russell Reynolds Associates get the most out of teamwork.

ORPHEUS: ALL FOR ONE, ONE FOR ALL

In the world of music, it is often said that a pianist plays the piano, a violinist plays the violin, and a conductor plays the orchestra. Traditional orchestras reduce individual musicians to cogs in a huge music-making machine, and isolate them from one another. Similarly, traditional business teamwork tends to focus primarily on interactions that improve efficiency at points where the activities of various employees come into direct functional contact. In many cases, teams serve only to report work results and provide information to the established management hierarchy. Broader idea sharing and decision-making authority are rarely part of the picture.

In Orpheus, we take an altogether different approach. While each of our members assumes full responsibility for his or her performance, the orchestra functions as a cross-communicative team of equal experts who develop and implement common goals and outcomes. Since teams begin with individuals, the first step we take to build effective teams is to give each member clear and concrete responsibility for contributing his or her ideas and expertise to the team's work. We choose team members based on the team's objectives, and we consider it essential that everyone accept a uniform, if subjective, benchmark for quality on each and every project. In our experience, if even one team member fails to buy in to that benchmark, our basis for effective teamwork is undermined, our ability to maintain our standards is eroded, and the entire group's performance is risked.

Building teams out of individuals, and basing our teamwork on clearly defined individual responsibilities, gives us the ability to set and maintain group standards. It also prevents our reliance on teams from becoming a way for anyone in the organization to escape responsibility for actions and choices. Says New York University management professor Bill Starbuck, "I use Orpheus as an example of what it takes to have real honest teamwork. Among other things, it says that it's a lot harder to have successful teamwork than the *Harvard Business Review* would have you believe. It takes a long time and a lot of mutual respect. They've had very little personnel turnover, which I think is essential."

Employee Responsibilities, Team Objectives

In our experience, effective teamwork requires a supportive organizational structure, which we achieve by giving our teams clear roles, significant responsibilities, and real authority. We also believe that to foster effective teams, an organization must give its employees opportunities to learn important team-based skills, such as how to cross organizational boundaries, support and complement one another, and function as generalists.

John Lubans, deputy university librarian at Duke University, has spent years studying the ways we develop and deploy self-managing teams.

According to Lubans, there are both structural and cultural reasons why teamwork works so well for Orpheus:

We start with individuals:

- Members' team roles are stated, agreed upon, and understood.
- All members invest an equal amount of time doing *real* work in the team.

Our team objectives cross over traditional boundaries:

- *Outcomes*, not reporting lines, drive the purpose of the team.

Our team members support and complement one another to produce outcomes:

- Members pay attention to *how* they work together.

We develop clear structures for teamwork:

- The purpose and mission of each team is clear and understood by every team member.
- Deadlines are stated and respected.

And, finally, we give institutional priority to team resources and teamwork skills:

- Teams receive demonstrable support from the organization.
- Each team in our organization understands its interdependence with other teams and does everything possible to support those other teams.
- Our teams are accountable to the organization and its leaders.[4]

Crossing Boundaries

In Orpheus, we do not allow the working process of our teams to be defined or circumscribed by reporting lines, technical expertise, or the functional job concerns of individual team members. We have discovered that these factors tend to hinder the development of true company-wide collaboration, and we believe that our capacity to prevent them from interfering with the internal dynamics of our teamwork is one of the distinctive strengths of our organization. Indeed, we constantly break the greatest of all orchestral taboos: Each of our musicians openly and directly makes suggestions to colleagues who play other instruments.

Violist Nardo Poy describes the state of teamwork in traditional orchestras: "If I were playing principal viola in, say, the New York Philharmonic, I couldn't turn to the timpani player and say, 'By the way, it's a little behind,' or 'It's too loud.' There's a protocol, and it would not be my role to do that. As a matter of fact, he'd probably tell me, 'Shut up, you mind your own business. Only the conductor tells me.' "

In contrast, during Orpheus rehearsals string players routinely voice opinions about woodwind articulation, percussionists argue with string players about bowing, and everyone discusses phrasing, balance, and nuance. (Guidelines for this communication are an important part of the Orpheus Process, and will be discussed in detail in chapter 7.) This ability to cross organizational lines and boundaries is critical; it makes it possible for individual members of Orpheus to take direct personal responsibility for product quality, to share and rotate leadership roles fluidly, and to support and complement one another fully.

Support and Complement

Our management process is team based as well and can be viewed as a supple expression of individual creative energies, combined and configured in myriad working groups in which each employee supports and complements other employees. Why? Time after time, we've seen that teams—when given clear and substantive responsibilities, as well as the necessary authority, support, and resources—get the very best out of our members, who come to respect each other's ideas and draw on each other's expertise.

In addition to the factors we have already discussed, there are three other important advantages to team-based management. On the most basic level, teams help us compensate for the natural ebbs and flows of employee energy and engagement in their jobs; when one person begins to fade, others step in to maintain the team's momentum. Teams also help us draw out the very best in each individual. Everyone in Orpheus is a superbly talented specialist, but teamwork is what motivates each individual in our organization to reach out to colleagues. Our team-based environment challenges and stimulates each of us, ensuring that Orpheus makes full use of our available human resources and intellectual capital. Finally, a positive and very real pressure to perform at the highest level drives everyone in our organization, because any individual failure affects everyone else and, ultimately, the quality of our products.

Our experience mirrors that of many other companies—members of self-directed and self-managed teams are more committed to their work and more committed to their organizations.[5] It takes more than applying the labels "self-directed" and "self-managing" to achieve results, however. According to organizational development consultant Barbara Kelly, "The move to self-directed teams requires changing not only the attitudes of people, it requires changing the organizational structure, information patterns, rewards and compensation systems, and the whole concept of career paths. With self-directed teams, employees require a lot of training in team skills. They need cross training in different functions, and they require much greater business training so that they can understand the impact of their actions on the organization."[6]

We foster an interdependent environment by relying heavily on project-oriented, ad hoc teams that constantly form and change, providing us with the ability to shift resources, refocus priorities, and utilize employee expertise to meet our most pressing and timely needs.

Relying on Ad Hoc Teams

In our experience, the best teamwork occurs when employees are asked to meet challenges that require diverse expertise and shared responsibility. Since these types of challenges and opportunities tend to emerge suddenly and unexpectedly, most of our teams are ad hoc; team members join and leave, as conditions in the organization and the market change.

Successful ad hoc teams pull together employees with the necessary experience, leadership skills, or untapped perspectives from throughout the organization, and empower them to make decisions that will achieve company-established objectives and outcomes based on their collective knowledge. In Orpheus, working groups of musicians, operating within a coordinating framework of permanent committees, form and disband from project to project. Management teams assemble to solve problems or respond to opportunities across departmental and organizational boundaries. All of these groups develop their own processes, internal roles, priorities, and goals.

Relying primarily on ad hoc rather than permanent teams gives us the flexibility to take advantage of multiple opportunities at the same time, and we often simultaneously deploy groups to several cities around the world. In one week in October 2000, for example, a team of Orpheus musicians coached the Orchestra of the National Conservatory of France in Paris; another team of musicians and administrators conducted a demonstration of the Orpheus Process for hospital executives and trustees at a conference in Chicago; and a third group stayed in New York to rehearse for upcoming concerts, teach Orpheus leadership techniques at Baruch College's Zicklin School of Business, and work on operating plans for the coming year.

Our marketing task force, which was active for an eight-month period in 1998, provides a good example of an ad hoc Orpheus team in action. Like most orchestras, Orpheus has faced intense competition from the constantly expanding universe of entertainment options throughout the past decade and, by the mid-1990s, we were confronted with significantly declining markets for our concerts and recordings. Within our organization, a broad consensus formed around the need to develop a long-term, strategic approach to marketing.

In response, the board asked one of its members, Infinity Broadcasting cofounder Michael Wiener, to assemble an ad hoc team of musicians, managers, trustees, and outside volunteers with special expertise. Those recruited to help included the head of an advertising agency, a corporate sponsorship consultant, direct marketing and PR specialists, and a market researcher. Within six months, the team, working under Wiener's leadership, developed and launched our first strategic marketing plan, based on methodical market research and substantial input from the musicians.

The marketing task force was built around a clear, specific objective and drew upon diverse experience and knowledge that was not available in any of our existing permanent teams. Looking back, it's clear that its work had a profound and long-term impact on our market position. Among its innovations and accomplishments were:

- A successful rebranding of Orpheus, including the creation of a new logo, print and radio campaigns, a Web site, and other promotional and imaging materials.
- The strategic decision to link educational activities with concerts to build new audiences.
- The creation of a professional marketing department including in-house staff and outside contractors.
- The launch of a new popular weeknight Carnegie Hall concert series to attract new and broader audiences.

- The development of a continuing network of volunteer professional marketing advisers for the organization.

The results of these initiatives have been dramatic. During the past three years, ticket sales to our flagship Carnegie Hall series have doubled. Newspaper, radio, and TV coverage of our concerts, recordings, and educational programs increased substantially, and this higher public profile has contributed directly to a 40 percent increase in our per concert price in North America, Europe, and Asia—despite generally shrinking attendance figures for classical music performances in each of those markets.

While ad hoc teams in Orpheus are given resources, authority, and a great deal of autonomy, we are careful to require that they function within the overall framework of our organization's mission, governance structure, operating plans, and collaborative environment. As in any organization, some matters are best handled by one of our permanent structures for group decision making. Therefore, we regularly review our overall organizational needs to assess if an objective or outcome should be assigned to an ad hoc or permanent team.

Utilizing Permanent and Formal Teams

To encourage self-directed and self-managing behavior around all of our decisions, we have created several permanent and formal teams with authority and responsibilities for areas that need annual, continuous, or repeated review. Each of these teams has a clear structure and set of responsibilities, leadership positions responsible for facilitating the team's work (which may be shared and rotated), and terms for its members.

For example, a special permanent committee of musicians, composed of three members elected for one-year terms, is responsible for selecting the concertmaster for each piece we perform (chapter 4 describes the concertmaster's key leadership responsibilities). This committee consists of two violinists, since the concertmaster is the section leader of the violins and represents that instrumental group (by far the largest one in the orchestra) in leadership cores, and one nonviolinist, since the concertmaster also has special responsibilities that affect everyone in the orchestra and, ultimately, plays a large role in shaping the final musical product. In addition to considering individuals who volunteer for the concertmaster positions, the committee solicits input from the orchestra's membership and consults closely with our artistic directors, who are also elected by the full orchestra and function collectively as another permanent formal team.

Our board of trustees and administration also accomplish a significant portion of their work through permanent teams, organized around major areas of ongoing responsibility such as budget and finance, fund-raising, recruitment, governance, long-range planning, and marketing.

Permanent teams must have clear responsibilities, just as employees do. For example, annual objectives for each of our board committees are set by the board's executive committee (which is made up of the chairs of each of the board's teams) after input from musicians and management; these objectives are then ratified by the full board. Similarly, the team objectives of the three artistic directors are important elements in our annual operating plan, which our administrative team develops after soliciting input from both musicians and trustees.

Company Objectives, Team Responsibilities

Even in a supportive environment like ours, successful teamwork is not a foregone conclusion. Musicians must work especially hard to maintain a spirit of teamwork, given their highly specialized skills and the compartmentalized nature of their training and experience outside our organization. Therefore, we devote considerable attention to developing teamwork skills among our members, rotating leadership, and offering opportunities for learning and growth whenever possible. But in the final analysis, a great deal comes down to the willingness of individuals to take responsibility for effective teamwork. Flutist Susan Palma-Nidel says: "There are so many variables. Sometimes you have the sense that people just come in to play their gig, and sometimes you really have a sense of everyone working together."

Each member of our organization is expected to make ongoing contributions to one or more teams, based on his or her expertise. There are many ways individuals can contribute to our team decisions and projects, and not all are as direct as advocating an interpretive idea about a piece of music in the middle of a rehearsal. However, the nature of specialized expertise requires us to develop teams of genuine equals that share information and the power to make decisions. No one person can possibly have the answer to every issue that faces our organization; horizontal teams leverage every person's and department's insights and skills, and integrate them for the organization's benefit.

Horizontal teams also give us valuable tools for including and fully engaging members, even when they are only able to devote limited amounts of time to our projects. For example, when cellist Eric Bartlett, a member of Orpheus since 1983, became associate principal cellist of the New York Philharmonic, he was forced to scale back his participation in our concerts, but he remained an integral member of our organization by making regular contributions to ad hoc teams (dropping in on rehearsals to give feedback to his colleagues) and formal permanent teams (serving on the executive committee of the board of trustees). Even when he is touring the world with the Philharmonic, Bartlett meets composers, young musicians, and academics to discuss Orpheus and exchange ideas.

Creating Generalists in Teams of Specialists

The trend toward workplace specialization, as old as the assembly line, continues to accelerate every day. It seems that the greater the potential of individual employees to add value through knowledge (a defining characteristic of the contemporary economy), the greater the focus on hiring and training a workforce dominated by specialized expertise. As a result, specialists, who tend to view their organizations' activities primarily through the narrow prisms of their specialties, increasingly dominate today's large corporations. Yet, the contemporary business landscape is defined by rapidly shifting marketplaces, constant technological revolution, and sudden changes in internal structures. Companies that encourage their employees to apply specialized knowledge, experience, and perspective to the "big picture" enjoy a significant competitive advantage over companies made up of people who are not allowed to grow beyond the narrow confines of their specialties.

But realizing this advantage requires companies to encourage their specialists to also function as generalists, and though many workers have the skills necessary to specialize and generalize, few companies offer incentives for their workers to use both sets of skills. Many companies create unintentional obstacles, or even deliberate barriers, that prevent their employees from becoming generalists. Even companies that recognize the capacity of their employees to understand how their specialized work fits into overall product quality often assume that these workers cannot usefully contribute their knowledge and experience to other areas within the organization.

In a traditional orchestra, the conductor is the designated generalist—the only person onstage authorized to make interpretive choices and the person exclusively responsible for shaping the musical product. In Orpheus, we have no designated generalist, and everyone in the organization has the opportunity, and responsibility, to be involved in broad "big picture" decisions.

Of course, each person approaches these generalist roles from a background of specialization. Each member of the orchestra has devoted decades to learning a single instrument, mastering its technical requirements and repertoire. Says violinist Martha Caplin, "We're all specialists, that's the beginning of the discussion. When I talk to another performer or another musician in the group, it's on an equal level. It's absolutely crucial that we all have that attitude."

But since we divide up the conductor's designated generalist role among our twenty-seven members, we have no alternative but to depend on each specialist to develop a generalist's knowledge of the music. In a traditional orchestra, the musicians learn only *their* parts; in Orpheus, the musicians are expected to learn the entire score; that is, their parts *and* everyone else's parts. We use teams to integrate these perspectives and apply a wide range of knowledge to our performances. But our members never allow their ability and inclination as generalists to interfere with the specialized requirements of instrumental performance. As pianist Richard Goode observes, this kind of involvement leads to a better product. Says Goode, "The members [are] intimately involved in the process, and . . . each one knows the score terribly well. This makes the whole experience terrific."

It also creates an enormously versatile reserve of talent and ability for the entire team, and allows the orchestra to respond quickly and effectively to crises. Often, a company can be paralyzed when a key decision maker or specialist leaves or is unavailable at a critical moment. By developing general knowledge in our specialists, we consistently meet such challenges. For example, on the way to a concert in Clinton, New York, French horn player Bill Purvis missed a left turn at Albany and ended up several hours away before realizing his mistake—at 7:30 P.M., thirty minutes before the concert was scheduled to start. The orchestra faced an especially critical problem because the concert featured Haydn's Symphony no. 44, which is famous for its intricate and difficult horn parts. Bassoonist Frank Morelli quickly took the score and, after a fast perusal, announced that he thought he could transpose the missing horn part and cover it adequately on the bassoon. Morelli went to work and, with assistance from the other horn player, adapted the part within minutes. The orchestra was on stage by eight o'clock, and the performance was a great success.

Many of our members have developed areas of specialized expertise such as baroque music performance, collaboration with contemporary composers, and the creation of concert programs for young children. Many are professors at conservatories or pursue pure research; others specialize in fund-raising or entrepreneurial ideas. Each of those additional specialties is immensely valuable to the organization as a whole; together, they provide a rich knowledge resource for the group.

Our structure encourages each member to contribute his or her specialized skills to achieving our strategic objectives through formal and informal teamwork. Our members are constantly encouraged to pitch in when and wherever they think they can, and each member therefore has the opportunity to play a role in every aspect of the life of the orchestra by suggesting repertoire ideas, offering opinions about marketing, recommending soloists and composers, helping recruit board members, reviewing the annual operating budget, designing educational programs, and participating in fund-raising.

This atmosphere of encouraging people to be both specialists and generalists also extends to the administrative staff. We have consistently found that people who demonstrate the capacity to absorb intense amounts of knowledge in a specialized administrative sphere are also likely to possess the capacity and interest to participate in the organization as generalists as well. Of course, some people prefer to function only as specialists, and these people make important contributions to the organization. But by encouraging employees to take on both specialist and generalist roles, we tap into a huge reservoir of skill and talent and unleash a tremendous amount of creative energy and dedication, while reinforcing employee value and loyalty throughout the organization.

Encouraging each individual to work outside his or her specialty motivates our members to stay with the orchestra and remain engaged. According to Frank Morelli, "Orpheus has allowed me—and compelled me as well—to develop my own understanding of music and my knowledge of the repertoire, how it's put together, how to rehearse it, how to make it sound better from an outside sense instead of just the bassoon line. Being around the musicians of Orpheus and the process has caused me to become a better musician—a more knowledgeable, skilled, and I hope deeper musician than I might have been had I not been a part of that process."

Jon R. Katzenbach and Douglas K. Smith, authors of *The Wisdom of Teams*, believe that teams create high-performance organizations and that they are the best solution for companies facing today's most common performance challenges, including technological change, competitive threats, environmental constraints, and customer service. But high-performance teams require commitment. According to Katzenbach and Smith, "What sets apart high-performance teams, however, is the degree of commitment, particularly how deeply committed the members are to one another. Such commitments go well beyond civility and teamwork. Each genuinely helps the others to achieve both personal and professional goals. Furthermore, such commitments extend beyond company activities and even beyond the life of the team itself."

In Orpheus, we share a high level of commitment to our musical products, to the organization, and to one another. It's this widely shared responsibility that allows our teams to be effective and productive and helps us create the best music that we possibly can.

THE SAN DIEGO ZOO: FORMAL TEAMS, SHARED RESPONSIBILITY

Team power results from drawing together a diverse group of people who pool their skills and experience to further their organization's goals. Real teamwork gives every employee a share in and responsibility for a company's innovations and success, and when teams of diverse individuals are given real authority to make decisions and implement ideas, a company amplifies the motivational and skill levels of its employees.

The San Diego Zoo, founded in 1916, is among the best known in the world. Built on one hundred acres of mesas, hills, and canyons in San Diego's Balboa Park, the organization pioneered the shift from "living museum" zoos, populated by bored animals housed in confining, concrete cages with sturdy metal bars, to "environmental" zoos filled with large, natural enclosures, stimulating play areas for the animals, and simulated rain forests. The zoo's annual budget of $50 million (which includes 261,953 household memberships and more than 5 million visitors each year) and its international renown as a tourist attraction have a significant impact on the San Diego economy.

Starting in the late-1980s, the San Diego Zoo has undergone a remarkable organizational transformation, as difficult and challenging as that faced by any business. For decades, the zoo had been divided into fifty separate departments organized by function types such as maintenance, animal keeping, horticulture, and education. Although the system seemed to work smoothly, the strict delineation of departments and jobs created problems and inefficiencies. On a basic level, as David Glines, formerly a groundskeeper and now the head of employee development, recalls, "Sometimes I'd sweep a cigarette butt under a bush. Then it was the gardener's problem, not mine." Over the years, such basic problems systemically filtered into every area of the zoo.

This all changed when the zoo's executive director, Douglas Myers, began integrating self-managing work teams into the zoo's operations in 1987. Today, the entire organization is based on formal teams with shared responsibility. Every section of the zoo now works in teams, directed by different people from different departments, depending on the expertise that's needed.

Just as an aerospace manufacturer like Boeing might assign teams to each of its aircraft development projects—the 777 passenger jet or the innovative new X-32 experimental aircraft—the San Diego Zoo created project teams to manage each of the zoo's mixed animal enclosures. Each team is responsible for every aspect of the area, from maintenance to animal and plant care, and includes specialized staff including custodial staff, animal keepers, horticulturists, and even construction managers. These teams, which usually aren't any larger than twelve to fifteen people, have their own operating budgets and are totally responsible for how their budgets are spent.

The San Diego Zoo's horizontal teams maximize the benefits of teamwork by being extremely flexible and sharing responsibility. Each one is a group of people who decide *what* task needs to be done, *when* it needs to be done, *how* they're going to do the task, and *who's* going to do it. The expectations are clear. Members constantly pitch in where they are needed, unconstrained by their individual work specializations or job descriptions. It's not uncommon, for example, for a bird keeper to work with a groundskeeper to solve a problem with an exhibit's physical plant. Myers says, "When someone walks into an area, everyone on the team is expected to know what's happening in the team area. And it's everybody's responsibility to correct problems."

By moving in and out of different jobs, depending on the needs of the team, employees work together with the common goal of maintaining their area at the highest level. When the zoo first started using self-managing teams, a visitor could clearly see the impact: areas run by teams were consistently cleaner and neater than those still under the old management system; the signage was well maintained, and there was a palpable feeling of pride of ownership.

The difference was also obvious to Douglas Myers. As employees became more engaged in their jobs, and learned more about the other jobs and responsibilities within their teams, they became much more valuable to the organization and helpful to one another. Says Myers, "It's fun to watch everyone work together to come up with incredibly innovative ideas in their areas. When we [started] nighttime zoo during the summer, the Gorilla Tropics team was faced with a problem. The great apes are like people—they go into their area at the end of the day, have a snack, and go to bed. By the time five o'clock rolls around, they're out. The team responded to the challenge, working with the marketing department to put together a video of what the great apes looked like during the day. Then they would go live to the big bedrooms where the groups stay at night and let the people see behind the scenes. [The team] knew guests would [visit] their area and they didn't want to disappoint them."

Says Gary Priest, curator of behavior management, "We don't have profit sharing or stock options. But we do have a mission that virtually every employee—whether they work in food service, with the animals, or in research—understands and feels ownership of. If anything, I find that sometimes I have to rein in my people because they want to do more than they physically can."

RUSSELL REYNOLDS ASSOCIATES: TEAMWORK MEANS BETTER CLIENT SERVICE

There are hundreds of executive search firms in the United States, but few equal Russell Reynolds Associates. Founded in 1969 and headquartered in New York City, the company has grown to more than 270 recruiting professionals working in thirty-five offices around the globe. Russell Reynolds specializes in recruiting and placing high-level executives in positions at some of the world's top companies, including ABC, the National Football League, the Carlyle Group, United Technologies Corporation, Glaxo Wellcome, and the Royal Ontario Museum.

Russell Reynolds's reach is exceptionally broad; the company works in more than forty specialized industries and practices, including the Internet, technology, media, board services, health care, financial services, and industrial manufacturing and distribution. On average, Russell Reynolds conducts more than three thousand recruiting assignments each year; more than 40 percent of these are for chairmen, chief executives, chief operating officers, chief financial officers, chief information officers, and directors. More than 50 percent of all their assignments are for positions with annual cash compensation in excess of $200,000. In 1999 (the most recent year with audited figures), the firm's revenues totaled $230.9 million, which was a 21.7 percent increase over the previous year.

Focus on Informal Teamwork

What makes Russell Reynolds continue to grow and flourish, and outperform the competition? Though many factors contribute to the firm's success, the company's emphasis on informal teamwork, built on a firm foundation of personal responsibility and shared expertise, is one of the most important. By emphasizing, encouraging, and rewarding teamwork, Russell Reynolds Associates has created a unique environment where employees strive to help one another, with each individual doing whatever he or she can to win an assignment for the firm.

Every Monday morning in each one of the firm's offices, Russell Reynolds's employees meet to discuss the week's new assignments, which are printed and distributed to all employees. These meetings generate new ideas, candidates, and sources that enhance and expedite the firm's client service, while giving each employee the opportunity to seek help with troubled assignments. By sharing information about assignments with everyone, whether the news is good or bad, the company's ultimate success becomes much more likely.

Russell Reynolds also encourages regular conference calls and frequent impromptu meetings to create a constant stream of opportunities for employees to share information and experience. These interactions with other members of the team can be particularly fruitful. Says Richard Lannamann, head of Russell Reynolds's Investment Management Practice and an Orpheus trustee, "Some of the best ideas and the fastest starts result from getting together with my colleagues to brainstorm a project."

Setting the Stage for Teamwork

Russell Reynolds encourages frequent personal contact to promote teamwork, setting the stage in its New Associates Program, a training session that brings together new associates from all of the company's offices. The firm sponsors regular strategy meetings to increase contacts among associates, generate new ideas for the firm, and promote team building. Each of the company's forty-plus practice groups meet regionally several times a year and worldwide on an annual basis. Every two or three years, the company sponsors a global conference that draws all Russell Reynolds professionals together for team-building activities that emphasize employee interdependence and the development of social relationships.

Russell Reynolds provides clear guidelines for fostering teamwork day by day. For example, recruiters follow a unique, hard-and-fast rule: the first five telephone calls in pursuit of a new executive search assignment must be to colleagues within the firm. This keeps employees in frequent personal contact with colleagues throughout the organization. According to Peter Drummond-Hay, managing director at Russell Reynolds and the person in charge of the firm's professional services practice, developing internal networks across groups and regions facilitates the formation of diverse teams for specific projects and gives the company a clear advantage over the competition.

Drummond-Hay illustrates this assertion with a story about a search the firm conducted for a large, publicly traded retail chain. The client needed to look outside its own management ranks to recruit a new CEO, and they wanted to make sure that they drew candidates from Europe as well as North America. Russell Reynolds approached the search by putting together a team, enlisting professionals from its Paris, New York, Toronto, and Chicago offices, to make a presentation at the client's board meeting in Toronto. As it turned out, Russell Reynolds was the only executive search firm that brought a Europe-based employee to the meeting. Russell Reynolds won the contract. Says Drummond-Hay, "Our greatest competitive advantage is our culture of teamwork because it enables us to put the right people in front of the client."

Supporting Teams with Information

As companies expand, hire new people, and open new offices around the world, it becomes more difficult, but also more important, to foster effective horizontal teamwork. Russell Reynolds's ability to do so has been greatly enhanced by RRAccess, the company's proprietary global database, which contains more than 1 million separate records compiled in thousands of assignments. Organizational information, conversations with clients, sources, candidate backgrounds, and references—all of these go into RRAccess, which provides Russell Reynolds employees with "anytime, anywhere" access to vital corporate knowledge and is a critical tool for building teamwork and collaboration within the organization.

Many firms have databases chock-full of contact information similar in scope to RRAccess. But the Russell Reynolds Associates database also records failures, false starts, and dead ends as well as successes and triumphs. The company's emphasis on teamwork is so strong, and the feeling of trust among colleagues so deep, that recruiters willingly record every possible detail—good or bad—about assignments. As a result, individual Russell Reynolds employees can navigate efficiently through an extraordinary amount of information and rapidly extract candid, pertinent, detailed material about clients, companies, industries, candidates, and references, giving the firm a significant competitive edge.

Russell Reynolds employees use RRAccess as their central team-building structure. The database facilitates the creation of ad hoc teams throughout the organization by giving individual employees the capacity to rapidly identify potential team members within the company's sprawling global network.

Evaluating Individual Performance

Performance at Russell Reynolds is assessed through an extensive 360-degree evaluation process that invites the employee's colleagues to rate his or her teamwork skills and practices, and the extent to which he or she shares information and offers the benefit of experience. Assists—credits given to team members as recognition for participating in a successful assignment—are highly valued in the organization.

The Russell Reynolds executive committee meets twice a year to assess the performance of each recruiter, using performance evaluations, including the role that the employee played in assignments and the number of assists earned. Of course, employees get feedback on teamwork strengths and weaknesses, but more important, teamwork and assists play a role in determining compensation and promotions.

In addition, Russell Reynolds structures compensation in ways that foster teamwork rather than internal competition. According to Drummond-Hay, "Every firm talks about teamwork—it's a buzzword—so talking about teamwork isn't enough. Most firms in our business are to some extent or other commission-based, which tends to foster selfish behavior instead of teamwork. Our compensation system helps differentiate us. It's one of the reasons we can live teamwork rather than just say it."

Teamwork in Action

Shortly after research consultant Tim Holt joined the Russell Reynolds New York office, he was pulled into a project in the real estate group when the team was short-handed. The goal of the search was to find a property manager familiar with the leasing and negotiations for high-end, multiuse developments. Although the client was a major New York developer, it was clear that the best candidate for this position might not be found in New York, so Holt reached out to his colleagues across the country via telephone and e-mail. Within two hours, Holt had a list of the top fifty shopping facilities in the United States, from which he prepared a prospect list of twenty top property managers. Within five days, he was able to completely flush out the top talent in that market and create a shortlist of the best candidates.

Because the Russell Reynolds culture rewards teamwork and employees who share information, Holt's colleagues were more than happy to serve on his ad hoc team. This stands in sharp contrast to the information hoarding that often characterizes other search firms. Says Holt, "Had we not been able to do that quickly, working together as a team, we would probably have lost the attention and the confidence of the client, and been unable to progress along the path of the search."

PUTTING THIS PRINCIPLE INTO PRACTICE

Horizontal teams, made up of employees with diverse ideas and expertise, can accomplish far more than the sum of the efforts of individual employees.

By pooling resources to complete a task or accomplish a goal, teams benefit from rapid information sharing, a wide range of skills and experience, and broad-based employee ownership of the company's outcomes.

But, while many organizations play up their commitment to teams and teamwork, they often fail to grant teams the responsibility and authority they need to get their jobs done, and they tend to underestimate the importance of communication between teams. When teams malfunction, employees feel powerless and frustrated, and a poorly structured team can actually waste the company's time, money, and talent.

Five Steps for Encouraging Effective Teamwork

STEP 1: Create a team-oriented organization that values self-management. The founders of Austin, Texas–based natural foods supermarket Whole Foods decided to allow stores, and employees within stores, to manage themselves rather than manage the entire operation centrally. Self-managing work teams, divided into product areas such as bakery, seafood, and produce, do their own hiring, firing, goal setting, and training. New Whole Foods employees must be approved by at least two-thirds of team members, who base their judgment on the candidate's performance during a three-day probation period. Bonuses are distributed to Whole Foods employees based on team performance, and financial data is available so that teams can track progress toward performance goals. The company's overall performance has flourished; Whole Foods is the top-ranked natural foods chain in the nation.[7]

STEP 2: Charge horizontal teams with organization-changing goals. Siemens Nixdorf Information Systems of Paderborn, Germany (now known as Wincor Nixdorf), chartered a special team of young employees from throughout the company to work with top management on the long-term implications of emerging demographic trends and breakthrough technologies. Says team member Stacy Welsh, "Our role is to challenge the board.

They look to us for perspective."[8] The team brought a fresh perspective to organizational thinking that enabled the company to better anticipate coming changes in the marketplace and take action to meet them.

STEP 3: Encourage the development of informal teams. At the San Antonio, Texas–based insurance company USAA, core groups charged with developing and introducing new initiatives into the company are joined by Tag Teams, informal groups of volunteers who attend the core group's major meetings and take responsibility for communicating news about impending change to their home departments. Says regional pride adviser, Karen Bredfeldt, "Tag Teams provide a reality check. The people on these teams are customer service reps. Their bottom-line concern is: 'How will this initiative affect customers?' And as advocates for their colleagues, they tend to ask hard-nosed questions. They also make sure that the company addresses issues that breed fear and insecurity: redesigned jobs, new managers, new functional areas. After meetings, Tag Team members are back on the job. This proximity to colleagues allows for lots of informal communication. Involvement, not containment, is the way to minimize disruption."[9]

STEP 4: Cross-train employees. When company management asked employees at AES Corporation's Deepwater power plant, located just outside Houston, Texas, to question the way they were doing business, employees reorganized the plant into teams, which they called "families" to underscore the responsibility of each individual to contribute to the team's work. Organized around different areas of the plant—for example, the turbine family, the scrubber family, and the boiler family—each family consists of workers who are cross-trained to learn each other's jobs, and who rotate their roles from day to day. The changes, which were designed to maintain a reasonable level of plant efficiency in spite of employee absences, actually increased plant utilization from 85 to 100 percent, while removing two layers of management. The company's top executives got into the act as well. All AES executives are required to spend a minimum of one week each year working in one of the company's power-generation plants. These executives learn every job in the plant, from tending boilers to loading coal and cleaning fouled equipment.[10]

STEP 5: Provide team resources. Just like the businesses that employ their members, teams need basic resources to survive and prosper. Here are some of the essentials:

- **Time:** Employees have to be given the time necessary to dedicate themselves to team meetings and other activities.
- **Facilities:** Teams have to have a place to meet.
- **Training:** Not every employee is a natural collaborator. All employees should receive training in teamwork and team building.
- **Money:** Teams should have sufficient budgetary authority to put their initiatives into practice.
- **Authority:** Decision-making authority is the most essential resource of all. Teams need to have—and to know they have—a real impact on the organization and its employees, vendors, customers, and clients.

Potential Traps and Land Mines

- **Vertical teams that draw on only one department's expertise.** When there's a problem with a product or process, it's natural for the responsible department to form a team to address the issue and solve it. But vertical teams such as these often miss out on the benefits of inviting employees from other departments to provide their own unique perspectives, and decisions are based on an inherently limited and biased set of data. Bringing in people from other departments often introduces new ideas, fresh perspectives, and different approaches. A team of product designers, for example, might greatly benefit from the input of salespeople—the employees who are closest to customers and know their needs and desires—by way of inviting them to join their team.
- **Groupthink.** Groupthink is the tendency of the members of any group of people, whether a project team or a committee, to conform to the opinions

and feelings prevailing in the group. Imagine a typical example where a roomful of managers all nod their heads in agreement, none expressing their own personal reservations, as a senior executive lays out her plans for introducing a new product. Groupthink can seriously undermine the value of teamwork to any organization. The antidote is open communication. Instead of pushing away, excluding, or assuming there are no alternative points of view, invite them, and encourage respectful but frank discussion of their relative merits.

- **Aggressive employees who hijack the team process.** For whatever reason—to impress management, create a power base, or try to get ahead—there are people in most companies who are focused on manipulating team processes to their advantage. Such people are generally aggressive, loud, and forceful, and they will often stop at nothing to get their way, including pressuring coworkers and shouting down opposition. It's important to not let such behavior go unchallenged, and to encourage those who aren't participating actively in the team process to become more involved. If the aggressive behavior continues, the employee may have to be asked to leave the team.
- **Teams that outlast their reason for being.** Organizational processes tend to maintain the status quo. All too often, team members become so accustomed to meeting on a regular basis and working closely with one another that even when the original problem is solved and the team's goals are met, the team continues, fishing for a new purpose. No team should exist without clear direction or goals, and when teams accomplish their objectives or complete their assigned tasks, it is best to disband them in a very public way. A party or rewards ceremony is a perfect way to celebrate the team's accomplishments, highlight the contributions of the team's members, and announce the end of the team's existence.

Although much has been made of teams and teamwork in business in recent years, the reality is that few organizations build teams with diverse expertise or give teams much in the way of real responsibility and authority, and thus defer to managers to make most decisions. As the examples of teamwork within Orpheus, the San Diego Zoo, and Russell Reynolds Associates demonstrate, teamwork can be an extremely powerful tool for harnessing the expertise of employees, especially when complex decisions must be made within a short time frame.

7

Learn to Listen, Learn to Talk

> It is ironic, but true, that in this age of electronic communications, personal interaction is becoming more important than ever.
>
> —REGIS MCKENNA, CHAIRMAN, THE MCKENNA GROUP

Information is power. This maxim has long been part of the organizational DNA of most companies and the managers who run them. As we discussed in the preceding chapter, information must be widely and openly available if it is to be exploited with maximum effectiveness. However, effective communication within organizations can hardly be taken for granted, in view of the substantial roadblocks and barriers that are built into dialogue between workers and management, among various interacting teams, and among all the stakeholders in a successful enterprise.

In traditionally structured corporations, hierarchies tend to harness the flow of information to evaluate, limit, and control employees, often for political rather than purely business reasons. On the other hand, knowledge workers tend to function poorly in environments defined by organizational control and constraint. Conversely, these workers tend to flourish in open communicative environments, where information and ideas flow up, down, and around the organization.

Because Orpheus empowers individual musicians and brings them together in self-managed horizontal teams, we have been forced to develop a profoundly original model of organizational communication. Finding ways for individuals with diverse professional backgrounds and organizational perspectives to communicate effectively is a constant challenge, which we meet by encouraging—and insisting—that everyone in the organization speak his or her mind, openly and honestly. Our communication is multidimensional, with information constantly flowing back and forth between every member of the orchestra and within and across our teams, regularly crossing the boundaries that stifle communication in most other organizations. Because our musicians depend on one another for direction, this ability to communicate across traditional boundaries is critical to the success of our products.

Each Orpheus rehearsal provides a remarkable opportunity to observe open and honest communication between individuals and teams in action. The guidelines we have developed to foster this exceptionally communicative environment have immense value and applicability to any organization.

THE PRINCIPLE

Traditional business communication is a formal and fairly rigid process that reflects and reinforces strict hierarchies, bottom-up reporting, and top-down decision making. By slowing down and tempering the exchange of important information, and excluding employees whose job descriptions or specialized knowledge do not seem related to the aspect of a project under discussion, formal presentations and written memoranda often control and sometimes inhibit the expression of ideas.

Free and unfettered communication is the best way to ensure that a company's full resources are brought to bear on organizational decision making.

This requires employees to learn to listen to each other and make a commitment to try out other employees' ideas; and to learn how and when to offer expertise and input to colleagues. When employees feel encouraged–and competent–to engage in open two-way communication about their company's products and services, innovative ideas are developed faster and potential problems are identified sooner. To achieve these results, each individual must take responsibility for mastering and balancing both listening and talking skills.

In Orpheus, we have developed a communication process based on the premise that every individual brings equal, if specialized, value to our organization. Each person and team is a unique hub in a network of respectful, two-way communication built on listening as well as talking, and employees must take personal responsibility for both as a fundamental part of their jobs. In our experience, anything less than respectful, two-way communication strangles the flow of information and inhibits new ideas that can improve product quality and add value.

Companies that open up their communication processes can expect the following:

- Increased worker creativity, and a flow of innovative ideas and suggestions

- Increased team productivity and improved morale

- An enhanced organizational ability to rapidly adapt to changing market conditions

- More honest and meaningful communication with clients and customers about their needs, which can be incorporated into product development

Opening up communication within a business requires real commitment on the part of management to identify and break down unnecessary barriers that constrain employees. In the sections that follow, you'll see how we at Orpheus and chip maker Intel have responded to this challenge.

ORPHEUS: TALKING AND LISTENING AS EQUAL PARTNERS

Orchestral musicians are trained from an early age to confine their professional speech to extremely narrow channels and restricted circumstances. Like orchestra conductors, many managers train their employees to limit idea sharing to special brainstorming sessions and make it clear that, for the sake of efficiency, employees are expected to confine their input at meetings or on teams to their direct areas of responsibility. Talking, the most basic and essential form of expressive communication, does not come naturally to the members of all too many organizations.

Our process requires an open environment and, to ensure that each member will have a voice on all issues, we have a simple policy: no topic, no matter how sensitive or controversial, is out of bounds for open discussion. Every member is encouraged and expected to express his or her point of view on matters ranging from artistic development and our business plan to decisions concerning personnel and which outside soloists we will perform with. Each person is responsible for communicating what he or she liked and didn't like about the previous night's concert, how the next performance can be improved, and what kinds of projects we should tackle in the future. There are long, involved conversations about the details of musical interpretation: whether the melody of a particular movement should be played softly and sweetly or in a more assertive style; how to balance the different instrumental voices; how slow or fast each piece should be played. We use the same basic communication guidelines for long-term strategic issues and short-term product decisions.

Of course, if everyone in an organization—especially an orchestra—is constantly talking, not much information can actually be communicated. To open the way for meaningful two-way communication, learning how, and when, to listen is at least as important as learning how to talk. Employees who have been heavily conditioned by years of experience in hierarchical workplaces, where listening to top-down direction is second nature, often need to develop their balance skills before they can function comfortably and effectively in an open and communicative environment.

We have found that hiring and retaining individuals who have a genuine interest in their fellow workers' points of view are vital to maintaining effective, two-way communication throughout our organization. In Orpheus, the responsibility for listening is not simply an imposed task; we all share a real desire to learn from our colleagues' experiences. We seek to build on this natural inclination by offering individuals the opportunity to develop the skills to lead and focus teamwork and decision making in an open and efficient manner. This collective ferment of talking and listening leads directly to our demonstrated capacity to make decisions in a fast, disciplined, and unified way—and, as you'll see in chapter 8, to build organizational consensus.

To create the open communication needed for effective teamwork, we have developed ground rules for respecting employee expertise, an organization-wide understanding of the appropriate language and time frame for idea sharing, and a system for filtering ideas. These are designed to allow us to remain focused on outcomes rather than communication and to reinforce our commitment to trying out new ideas, from any member on any issue, if the idea could potentially help us reach our objectives.

Respecting Others

The Orpheus Process is built on the conviction that each member contributes uniquely valuable skills and knowledge and that individual abilities should be fostered, encouraged, and celebrated for the organization's benefit through an open and communicative environment. Says New York University management professor Bill Starbuck, "This translates to mutual respect. They believe that the other people have a lot to contribute and that they must rely on them to do well." As violinist Martha Caplin puts it, "We're all giving to each other what we do so specially well. It's our differences that make the creative process so essential to Orpheus."

Just as we value clearly defined roles (as discussed in chapter 4), we also carefully define the skills needed for respectful communication within our organization. Our musicians must be willing and able to suspend disbelief and seriously consider other points of view throughout the process of developing our musical products, since product quality comes first and foremost for the entire organization. Violinist Ronnie Bauch cites two essential qualities needed by every Orpheus member to balance listening and talking: self-confidence and self-discipline. "There have been many fine musicians who have played with us for three years without saying a word, until they finally worked up the courage to make a verbal contribution. On the other hand, there are people who jump right in and make comments that demonstrate a lack of discipline; they're speaking without concern for what's being worked on."

According to Harvard professor Richard Hackman, Orpheus is rare in "recognizing, dealing directly with, respecting, and exploiting—in the best sense of the word—the differences among members. They recognize that people have different talents, skills, and knowledge bases, and they turn to the people with relevant expertise." This organization-wide respect for skill gives us an advantage in designing our products and delivering them efficiently and effectively.

Ground Rules for Respectful Criticism

Any organization striving to achieve innovation and excellence, without a controlling central authority, requires employees who are able to offer and accept a constant stream of respectful criticism. This is far from easy. Says cellist Eric Bartlett, speaking of his Orpheus experience: "Since there's no conductor, in order for us to sound good we have to do a lot of incredibly difficult work. We have to criticize each other. Musicians aren't crazy about being criticized, even by a conductor, and a lot of musicians are really uncomfortable with being criticized by colleagues. It has to be done in a way that won't come back and land in your lap."

What makes a respectful climate possible in Orpheus is the shared knowledge that all of our musicians function at the highest level of professional skill, and that each one is dedicated to the excellence and perfectibility of our products. Says bassoonist Frank Morelli, "It's normal for anyone to feel a twinge of discomfort when someone criticizes him or her, even for members of Orpheus. But I always remind myself that Orpheus exists largely because of the unique qualities of the players. So, if anyone in the group has something to say to me about how I played something, I look at it as a gift, a free lesson. Why? Because I know I'm in the presence of someone I have the greatest respect for. I feel there's a lot I can learn."

Working from this foundation, we have identified three behaviors that sustain our climate of mutual respect and function as ground rules for our members:

1. **Being on time.** Punctuality may sound trivial, but it is a fundamental way for each individual to show respect for colleagues. No one's time is more or less important than anyone else's. Making the best possible product in a collaborative environment requires the full participation of each member—and a basic sense of fairness and equality.
2. **Using language precisely.** Our members strive to avoid unnecessarily inflammatory or personally disrespectful criticism. We encourage criticism that focuses on solutions and uses humor to make its points; we discourage criticism that focuses on problems and employs mockery.
3. **Letting go of trivial issues.** Throughout the organization, we tend to reserve criticism for the issues that really matter, because of their impact

on product and quality. For example, when a member's performance at a concert falls below expectations, others typically refrain from raising the issues, on the assumption that the problem is isolated or transient. If recurrent issues arise, members do not avoid their responsibility to criticize, but the discussion focuses on how to improve performance, not on the mistakes.

Individuals in our organization also demonstrate respect for one another by not offering suggestions or ideas frivolously. We take responsibility for sharing ideas that may improve our collective performance, but we are also aware of the time required to properly consider and test a new idea, and we are therefore extremely disciplined about which ideas we put forth. On the other hand, when a member feels strongly enough about an idea to communicate it to the group, the idea is tested with full conviction. Everyone in Orpheus suspends disbelief while listening to others, and each individual in our organization remains open to other points of view—even those in direct conflict with our own preconceptions—to give all possible solutions a fair hearing.

Ideas, initiative, creativity, energy, passion—these are among the most vital qualities that any worker can contribute to his or her company. Individuals are most likely to contribute their best ideas and most essential talents to their jobs when they feel secure and self-confident. A respectful environment engages workers on a personal level, and employees who flourish in a respectful environment can have an enormous impact on product quality and customer satisfaction.

Forums for Communication

Communication thrives in a corporate culture that encourages honest, open, and impassioned expressions of different points of view, where nothing is papered over, no one feels stifled, and no idea goes unexamined. Along with this freedom, however, comes the responsibility to express opinions in a constructive way, and our members have learned to calibrate their communications based on the impact their knowledge will have on the organization at different stages in the decision-making process. Each one of our musicians is constantly making subtle and sophisticated judgments about how to maximize their contribution to the orchestra's product. An orderly process underlies our discussions, so that communication remains efficient and directly focused on harmonious resolutions.

Our commitment to identifying the best solutions has naturally led us to function as a meritocracy; Orpheus can best be viewed as a marketplace of constantly competing ideas, in which individuals and teams win over supporters based on information. No one is prevented from expressing an opinion, but there is no guarantee that any particular idea will be incorporated into decisions or gain support from colleagues, even when initiated or supported by designated leaders. As board member Ed Sutton puts it, "In Orpheus, each individual is empowered to have his own opinion and to have it heard—but not to act unilaterally."

Core groups can spend dozens of hours developing interpretive ideas about a piece of music, only to have them overturned and discarded after a few minutes of discussion in full rehearsal. A horn player, the chairman of a board committee, the finance director—everyone in the organization knows that their perspective may be questioned by anyone else in the organization, at any time, in the search for the best solutions.

Presenting Solutions, Not Problems

Over the years, we have learned that our communication and, ultimately, our performance improve when we use our marketplace of ideas to focus on developing solutions rather than just identifying problems. Says violinist Eriko Sato, "Fundamentally, I don't think everybody's opinion should be addressed at all times. There are certain places and times for certain things to be said—the appropriate moment. Everybody knows what's wrong, everybody can feel what's wrong—but do you have a solution? Do you know how to solve a problem?"

We depend on invested employees to offer solutions to organizational problems by working with permanent or ad hoc team members who are responsible for an issue. By fully engaging our pool of talent, we maximize our most powerful resource and give ourselves the capacity to solve unexpected problems in a fluid and efficient way. Everyone in our organization is encouraged to participate in any project to which they feel they can contribute, regardless of their job title, team assignments, or primary roles.

Several years ago, when Orpheus faced a communication breakdown and the musicians felt disenfranchised because key decisions were being made without their input, we solved the problem by creating formal teams whose members held explicit responsibility for representing diverse opinions from throughout the organization. Says violist Nardo Poy, "We were asking management to tell the board our concerns, and it never got further. Now that there is no filter between the board and the musicians—because we have members who go to the board meetings and participate with management—breakdowns like that won't happen again. The board keeps the lines of communication open, listens to our ideas, and tries to act on them."

Expressing ideas and listening to other points of view are essential elements of the Orpheus Process. By creating an environment where everyone is encouraged to talk to and listen to colleagues, we ensure a steady supply of good ideas; by maintaining clear leadership structures and individual responsibility for product and quality, we ensure that this communication is effectively integrated into our decision making.

Hiring Good Communicators

Cultivating a respectful business climate is much easier if a company can identify potential employees who are willing and able to communicate openly and honestly. In Orpheus, we use a collaborative hiring process that allows us to assess a candidate's capacity to work well in a collaborative environment. Candidates for most positions meet with a range of people throughout the organization so we will be able to consider the feedback of many specialized employees while observing how the candidate handles group dynamics and navigates diverse perspectives. Successful candidates are involved in shaping their own working environment from day one; some respond to the interviews with excitement and ideas, and often help redefine their job descriptions based on the skills and expertise they display in interviews.

The personnel-selection process particularly concerns cellist Eric Bartlett, because hiring decisions are one of the most important elements in sustaining our management style. Says Bartlett, "Orpheus is a group of highly skilled individuals who have been handpicked—without audition, because we feel that the audition process doesn't serve our purposes at all—for their abilities to lead, to follow, and to give and take criticism constructively. It is an extraordinary challenge to find all those social abilities in a highly skilled musician or administrator. People are selected with the expectation that you *can* put them all in a room together and they will treat each other as equals. We expect them to lead each other and to be led by each other without any problem."

A Responsibility for Good Communication

Finally, to ensure that communication flows freely throughout the organization, we devote considerable attention to making sure that each person in the group continues to take responsibility for productive and respectful communication. Each member, whether a designated leader or a follower, knows that withholding useful ideas or offering frivolous ones undermines his or her own performance as well as the orchestra's.

The ethos of mutual respect is so deeply ingrained in our culture that employees look forward to having their ideas challenged and improved upon by their peers. For violinist Eriko Sato, respect for her peers makes criticism one of the most rewarding aspects of her job. Says Sato, "I think that's what I actually live for—deep down you know that the audience can be easily manipulated in certain ways. I think that our colleagues are our purest critics." In an organization dedicated to perfectionism, mutual respect enforces high performance standards, often higher than current customer expectations.

Within the orchestra, members constantly, but informally, evaluate how new musicians fulfill their responsibility for listening and talking; no formal hearings, flurry of memos, or bureaucratic board of inquiry, just a simple, frank, and honest conversation. But, inevitably, some individuals cannot develop the skills to meet our guidelines for communication. In a watershed moment from our early history, one of our most gifted violinists was denied the role of concertmaster for being unable to deal respectfully with differences of opinion by balancing assertiveness with facilitation. An important principle was established—in Orpheus, disrespect and unbridled expression of personal ego are never tolerated, even if an individual brings substantial talents to the organization.

When there is a lack of respect in any organization, whether from the top down or from the bottom up, communication becomes inhibited and the transfer of information slows. Respect opens people up, encouraging them to communicate and bring their ideas and solutions to the attention of those who can implement them. According to Dr. Deborah Johnson, director of the Program in Philosophy, Science, and Technology for the school of Public Policy at the Georgia Institute of Technology, respect for employees is fundamental to the development of any successful organization, and there's much more to the process than simply treating employees well. Says Johnson, "It requires employers to recognize staff members as human beings with interests of their own and the right to make decisions about their lives."[1]

According to Faye Wilson, senior vice president for value initiatives and a member of the Home Depot board of directors, "The most basic value, particularly in a multicultural company and a multicultural society, is respect. It is the value that allows us to listen to other people, to welcome their ideas, and to respect their contributions. At the Home Depot, respect is something that's not just talked about, but practiced as well." Employees confirm that the respect they feel at Home Depot directly and positively impacts their work lives. Says one, "The environment here is best described as a feeling more than anything else. I have always been encouraged to think on my feet, come up with new ideas, and have the freedom to implement them. You can make a mistake without having a big hammer come down on you. It's part of the learning process."[2] Says Wilson, "When you have associates who feel respect, you are going to respect your customers, and that certainly has to translate into customer loyalty. I have to believe that we get a lot more sales because we respect each other and we respect our customers. That's very much a bottom-line item."

The Power of Talking and Listening

In the mid-1990s, Orpheus found itself in a difficult dilemma. Only 15 percent of our revenue-generating activities (concerts, recording sessions, and broadcasts) took place in and around New York City, home to our organization and all of our members; the remaining 85 percent of our work was spread out all over the globe. Near-constant travel created severe stress on our members and their families, and made it difficult for members to combine their work in the orchestra with other academic and performing opportunities.

From an organizational perspective, constant travel increased our cost of doing business, while eroding our ability to attract a solid base of support in any one market. Tellingly, focus groups we conducted in 1998 revealed that many of New York's classical music lovers thought that Orpheus was a German orchestra; during the preceding year, we had performed more concerts in Germany than in New York.

Reluctantly, our members began to vote "with their feet" by declining to sign up for more lengthy tours; this decline in member participation threatened our product quality and our brand reputation. Our business plan was not working.

Alarmed at this trend, in 1997 violinist Ronnie Bauch drafted a working paper designed to call attention to the problem and sketch out a potential solution, which he called *The Orpheus Institute*. The future outlined differed radically from the orchestra's then-existing business plan. *The Orpheus Institute* built a case for shifting our organizational priorities to give the orchestra a home base, create educational programs, and build loyal customers. It culminated by calling for the development of a permanent performance, teaching, rehearsing, recording, and research center for Orpheus in New York.

Although *The Orpheus Institute* dramatically underestimated the difficulties of achieving its objectives, and did not attempt to address many of the central business and financial issues related to the plan, the proposal quickly achieved its primary purpose—to become a catalyst for organizational change. In the best Orpheus spirit, *The Orpheus Institute* identified problems, proposed solutions, and galvanized discussions that ultimately led to far-reaching organizational changes. Much of the paper's effectiveness came from its use of important components of our communication process: It was the product of an individual taking personal responsibility for a broad organizational issue—the deep divide between our business plan and the objectives and aspirations of our musicians—and it focused on solutions.

In response, we formed a special ad hoc team of trustees, administrators, and musicians to consider structural changes to improve internal communications throughout the organization. Many of our present leadership structures—notably the artistic director positions and the representation of orchestra members on the board and its committees—resulted from the work of this informal team. Within a year, a special long-term planning committee of trustees, musicians, and managers began to dramatically improve our channels of communication within the organization and refocus our business plan around four newly agreed-upon organizational objectives:

1. More work in and around New York
2. Increased employee compensation
3. A strengthened role in education
4. A renewed commitment to involving everyone in the organization in decision making

As executive director, I began a major effort to shift the ratio of performances away from the road and toward the group's home in New York City. It wasn't an easy task; the marketplace was—and is—extremely competitive, and we were simultaneously trying to increase income in order to improve musician salaries, which had been frozen for many years.

In looking for solutions, we realized that the need to re-rehearse the same piece of music every time the group of members performing the piece changed was a critical problem. Our performance costs increase sharply with each rehearsal, yet these additional rehearsals did little to add value to our musical products. Our solution radically changed employees' responsibilities by implementing a seasonal contract designed to stabilize group membership and increase member participation. Through the introduction of the seasonal contract, our members are gaining many of the objectives outlined in *The Orpheus Institute*, but they are also giving up much of their traditional freedom to pick and choose which projects they will participate in.

The board and administration had heard the orchestra's desire to spend less time on the road loud and clear, but the orchestra then had to listen and eventually support our best idea for financially achieving that goal. To change the organization's long-held strategies and assumptions, *every* member of Orpheus had to listen seriously to the ideas put forth by others, and help incorporate them into solutions. By 2001, more than half of Orpheus's work was in and around New York, musician pay under the seasonal contract had grown by 40 percent, and our education program had grown from two to thirty-five activities each year.

As a result, everyone in Orpheus realizes that when they're shaping a musical program, they're also shaping a part of a large and complex business strategy, to which every member has contributed.

INTEL: A CULTURE OF CONSTRUCTIVE CONFRONTATION

Every day, we see fresh evidence that the rapidly accelerating pace of technological change is driving more and more organizations, and the people within them, to work faster and harder than ever before. This trend makes effective communication ever more important, especially in large corporations where many barriers to effective communication often exist. To be effective, corporate communication must be fast, complete, and honest—sometimes brutally so.

Nowhere is this more the case than at Intel Corporation, the Santa Clara, California–based company founded by the inventors of the microprocessor. A company with more than $29 billion in annual sales, Intel continues to dominate its competition with an 80 percent market share and a three-decade track record of technological innovation.

When Intel was founded in 1968, Gordon Moore and Robert Noyce decided to reinvent corporate culture. Noyce described the Intel environment as "a community of common interests . . . a cooperative venture [more] than an authoritarian structure—a community rather than an army. People came here because of their abilities, and we knew we would all prosper or fail together."[3] Moore and Noyce developed a work environment of equals, all focused on producing results.

Intel's result orientation—setting challenging goals, striving to execute flawlessly, and focusing on output—established a company-wide responsibility for outcomes and encouraged employee dedication to constructively confronting and solving problems. Constructive confrontation assumes that "yes-man" behavior is unproductive and that truth telling is more valuable to the company's bottom line than boosterism. Taking a critical perspective is every employee's responsibility at Intel, and employees are expected to assertively voice any disagreement with prevailing wisdom.

At Intel, employees are free to, and expected to, openly challenge the business and technical assumptions or proposals of their coworkers and managers. In fact, vigorously challenging ideas that don't make sense quickly became a trademark of Intel communication and its high-performance culture, as managers decided that competition required them to quickly identify and solve problems. Says Intel engineer Rick Lewelling, "You get your chance to say what you think. Disagreements can sometimes get emotional. But you get to the best solution, and everyone commits to that."[4]

The culture of constructive confrontation makes Intel a very different place to work than most other companies since, according to a survey of forty thousand Americans, 93 percent of employees regularly lie at work.[5] According to Cheryl Shavers, general manager for Intel's advanced technology operation, "If you're giving a presentation, anything you say can be challenged by anyone, regardless of your position in the company. At other companies, the senior staff say, 'Here's where we're going, here's what you need to know, good-bye.' At Intel, it's 'This is where we're going,' and everyone in the room jumps up and says, 'Why does that make sense?' It can be a feeding frenzy."[6] But because Intel has uniform guidelines for participation, employees and managers are able to work together to filter through the ideas and implement strategies.

Although he turned the reins of power over to president and CEO Craig Barrett several years ago, chairman Andrew Grove—the man most people think of when they hear the name Intel—is still very much an active part of the company who teaches and lives the virtues of constructive confrontation each workday. Says Grove, "At every facility, we have orientation programs taught by people like me—folks who have been around a while. We teach a bit about the company and the culture. I teach a class on how to initiate and manage constructive conflict. The real learning, though, comes on the job. When my people aren't confronting an issue, I confront them. I support them if that's what they need, but I make sure they confront [the issue]. When I see a chain of e-mail messages, I know people aren't confronting. When I see an e-mail with a big long tail floating across my screen, I tell people 'I'll stay the whole time in the meeting you need to have, but we've got to confront this.' "[7]

While constructive confrontation, open communication, and Intel's other distinctive workplace practices are second nature to established employees, they can be quite foreign to new hires who come from businesses where less forthcoming behavior is encouraged and rewarded. To solve this problem, Intel places great emphasis on its new employee orientation program. Starting before a new employee arrives at the office for his or her first day of work and seamlessly continuing in professional development training, the program ensures that every employee fully absorbs the company's values and integrates them into his or her work.

Meetings of Minds

Grove calls meetings "the medium of managerial work."[8] In his book *High Output Management,* he makes the case that meetings are crucial for communicating information and company experience to employees, for imparting a sense of how the manager prefers his or her employees to handle their responsibilities, and for facilitating group decisions. Instead of fighting meetings, or trying to do away with them altogether, Grove argues that meeting leaders should do everything in their power to make the time spent in them as efficient as possible.

According to Grove, there are two basic kinds of meetings: process-oriented meetings and mission-oriented meetings. Process-oriented meetings should be scheduled on a regular basis, to guarantee that they aren't pushed aside by pressing business priorities and, more important, encourage regular dialogue and feedback between supervisors and workers. These meetings provide opportunities for sharing knowledge and exchanging information, in one-on-one, project-wide, or cross-departmental forums.

One-on-one meetings between supervisors and employees ensure that individuals learn. According to Grove, "By talking about specific problems and situations, the supervisor teaches the subordinate his skills and know-how, and suggests ways to approach things. At the same time, the subordinate provides the supervisor with detailed information about what he is doing and what he is concerned about." In short, one-on-ones go a long way to facilitate regular, two-way communication between workers and managers to benefit employees, the organization, and its customers.

Staff meetings in Intel involve all of the people working in a department on a single goal, providing an opportunity for interaction among peers. Vice president and e-business director Sandra Morris's weekly "Go-No Go" meetings show how Intel utilizes staff meetings to give power to employees rather than supervisors. At the meeting, Morris asks whether or not each staff member has his or her piece of a project—quality assurance, customer support, information technology, or other responsibilities—in place, ready to go, on schedule. Those who answer "go" receive a nod of recognition from Morris. Those who answer "no go" are asked one additional question: "What do you need to make it a go?" According to Morris, "Honesty is critical. People need to see that when they say they've got a 'no go,' the response isn't 'Why not?' but 'What do you need?'" Using this approach, Morris's group created a secure, Web-enabled, customizable ordering system to handle $1 billion in company sales in only six months' time. The project met its $1 billion volume goal only fifteen days after the system went on-line.[9]

A final process-oriented meeting, Intel's operation reviews, allow employees to interact regularly across departments and projects. Such meetings include formal presentations by managers describing their work to staff in other parts of the company or who aren't in their immediate chain of command. Increasing communication between employees who work in different parts of the company transfers knowledge and lessons.

Intel also holds mission-oriented meetings designed to reach a specific goal, such as responding to an opportunity or problem. For these meetings to be successful and productive it is critical that the meeting's leader identify the precise purpose of the meeting and then determine and assemble the right ad hoc team and agenda. According to Grove, the size of mission-oriented meetings needs to be limited. "Keep in mind that a meeting called to make a specific decision is hard to keep moving if more than six or seven people attend. Eight people should be the absolute cutoff. Decision making is not a spectator sport, because onlookers get in the way of what needs to be done." When the meeting is completed, the meeting leader immediately sends out minutes summarizing the essence of the discussions, decisions made, the actions to be taken, and by whom.

By instituting a system of regular and ad hoc meetings emphasizing efficiency, any organization can create high-performance communication on par with Intel's model.

PUTTING THIS PRINCIPLE INTO PRACTICE

Few organizations effectively encourage wide-ranging and open communication that crosses departmental boundaries, job titles, and other artificial constraints in the pursuit of solutions for the organization, its clients, and its customers. Giving employees at every level the responsibility to talk and listen, and the respect their ideas deserve, creates an organizational culture focused on meeting challenges and capitalizing on opportunities, quickly and effectively.

Five Steps for Changing the Culture of Communication

STEP 1: **Make it safe to communicate.** Michael May, CEO of the Overland Park, Kansas–based computer training firm Empower Trainers & Consultants, believes that making it safe for associates to discuss their mistakes with managers and other employees improves performance. Says May, "If mistakes are hidden, they remain land mines." Associates at Empower are encouraged to post a Today's List of Mistakes form on their office doors. As each workday proceeds, associates fill in the form's seven numbered lines with their mistakes and display them for coworkers to peruse as they walk the halls. Mistakes are entered into a special database available to all associates for finding solutions and troubleshooting mistakes before they happen. To build trust and foster a safe environment for communicating important information, management promises to use the information for learning and not for employee evaluation.[10]

STEP 2: Create new forums for communication. When Tampa, Florida–based AmeriSteel became an open-book management firm—sharing its financial data with all employees instead of only a select few—management had to come up with new ways to communicate complex financial concepts to the company's employees. Chief financial officer Tom Landa distributed a customized board game to employees that explained the basics of the company's financial workings, and installed a series of electronic bulletin boards throughout the company's facilities. These bulletin boards, which are updated every two weeks, display the company's key financial data and indicators. Even the first page of each of AmeriSteel's twenty-one different division newsletters contains a presentation of company financial information.

STEP 3: Encourage and reward honest and open dialogue. At AGI, Inc., the Melrose Park, Illinois, nontraditional packaging designer and printer (recently merged with Klearfold to create a new company, the IMPAC Group), open and honest communication is everything. At AGI's monthly company-wide meetings, CEO Richard Block invites employees to ask any question, no matter how sensitive or potentially explosive it might be. To reinforce his invitation, Block gives the employee who asks the toughest question at each meeting a special award. As the winner of Avon Cosmetics' coveted Supplier Excellence Award an unprecedented twelve times, Block takes pride in the company's culture, designed to be, in his words, "an environment . . . for experimentation . . . that urges you to take responsibility for a problem instead of working to conceal it."[11] Block is convinced that promoting open debate and an open exchange of ideas gives AGI its competitive advantage.

Step 4: Be nonjudgmental. Jerry Hirshberg, founder and recently retired president of Nissan Design International, Inc., in San Diego, California, believes that both telling the truth and hearing the truth are critical elements of successful communication. Says Hirshberg, "Even people who don't mind telling the truth have mixed feelings about hearing the truth. It's like a chemical reaction: Your face goes red, your temperature rises, you want to strike back. Those are signs of the 'two D's': defending and debating. Try to fight back with the 'two L's': listening and learning. Many of the best ideas are communicated through whispers—in the hallway meetings that happen after the official meeting. That's because people worry about how the boss will react if they speak the truth. What's remarkable, of course, is that these whispered ideas are what companies are most hungry for. So the next time you feel yourself defending and debating, stop—and start listening and learning instead. You'll be amazed by what you hear."[12]

Step 5: Focus communication on product, not function. When employees communicate only within a department you risk fostering an us-versus-them attitude rather than a for-the-good-of-all attitude. As companies expand, the risk increases as the physical distance between employees increases. According to Jane Mount, executive vice president at New York City–based Bolt, Inc., an Internet-based communications forum for teenagers, employees started feeling disconnected from one another when rapid company expansion required groups of employees to move into new offices on separate floors. Bolt implemented a "hive mind" seating system that groups employee work spaces by project rather than function or department. Says Mount, "Because everyone is intermingled, they've adopted a common, overarching goal. And this isn't the goal of Bolt sales or Bolt marketing: It's the goal of Bolt, Inc."[13]

Potential Traps and Land Mines

- **Managers who ignore what their workers, clients, and customers are saying.** Managers get paid to know their business, but smart managers are aware that they don't know everything there is to know and that they can always learn something new from their employees and coworkers, as well as from clients, vendors, and customers. Managers who mistakenly believe that they know everything tend to talk too much while listening too little. One-sided communication results in directive monologue rather than a collaboration built of shared ideas, suggestions, and perspectives. Whether you're in a management position—or in any other position within an organization—listen as much as you talk, and incorporate others' ideas into your solutions. Record ideas that aren't pursued, so if conditions change or assumptions are wrong you can immediately incorporate them.

- **Fear.** The fastest way to shut down communication in an organization is to punish employees, formally or informally, when they speak candidly. Managers who snap at employees, dismiss ideas quickly, or publicly ignore employee contributions send the message that communication only serves to support their decisions. Worse, managers who threaten, intimidate, and coerce employees into supporting their decisions will lose the benefit of their employees' expertise—and often the employees themselves. Send a clear message to managers that hearing from their employees is one of their most important responsibilities, and that they will be evaluated on how well they listen.
- **Structural constraints to communication.** Even with the advent of voice mail and e-mail, some organizations continue to hinder communication more than they foster it. Rows of offices with closed doors, strict rules against people socializing on the job, and a lack of common areas constrain effective communication between employees. But this doesn't have to be the case; you can initiate organizational changes that will make communication a better, more effective experience for all involved. When Pitney Bowes Credit Corporation (PBCC) of Shelton, Connecticut, remodeled its offices a few years ago, managers decided to create a "town square" focused around the main hallway, now festooned with cobblestone-patterned carpets, a 1950s-style diner, street signs labeled Front Street, Wall Street, and Overlook Drive, and even a French-style café. The new

offices got employees talking with one another, trading ideas and insights. Says Matthew Kissner, PBCC's president and CEO, "We wanted a fun space that would embody our culture. No straight lines, no linear thinking. Because we're a financial-services company, our biggest advantage is the quality of our ideas."[14] Find the organizational constraints to communication in your business and, one by one, tear them down, replacing them with systems, processes, structures, and environments that enhance and encourage communication.

- **People who dominate discussion.** Some people are more assertive than others and can dominate discussions while inhibiting others from participating. When individuals continually dominate communication in your organization, you lose out on the ideas, suggestions, and feedback of employees who are less assertive or less willing to advocate for their ideas. Find ways to show that you appreciate employee ideas, and encourage everyone to be a part of the process. Try staffing teams so that less vocal employees with special expertise have a responsibility to speak up or assertive employees hold leadership or other roles that require them to listen rather than talk.
- **Meetings that are a waste of time.** Meetings are often considered a waste of time by those who attend them, perhaps deservedly so. Research indicates that more than half of all time spent in business meetings is wasted.[15] If you multiply the number of people in your organization by the amount of time they spend in meetings every year, which may exceed a third of some employees' time on the job, you can see that this can amount to an extraordinarily high cost in lost productivity. But, in most companies there are few ways better than meeting to communicate information and get things done. Find ways to reduce wasted time in meetings, such as setting limits on the time spent discussing a problem without also sharing background information and discussing solutions before a meeting is convened.

Most people are quite skilled at both talking and listening, but integrating and balancing the two are tricky, and effective communication in organizations involves equal measures of both. Open and honest communication is a basic responsibility of every member of Orpheus, and the active participation of everyone in our ongoing group discussion is essential to our organization's health and our capacity to function. As we saw in the case of computer chip–maker Intel Corporation, intellectual honesty between employees at every level of the organization creates a superior product. In the words of Intel chairman Andy Grove, "How well we communicate is determined not by how well we say things, but by how well we are understood."[16]

8

Seek Consensus (and Build Creative Structures that Favor Consensus)

Nothing astonishes men so much as
common sense and plain dealing.

—RALPH WALDO EMERSON

A company that does not involve its employees in solving thorny problems is failing to take advantage of its most important resource: its people. Achieving consensus—which comes from the Latin word meaning "shared thought"—doesn't require gaining the complete agreement of every employee or internal constituency for every aspect of every decision. Rather, consensus means reaching a broad level of internal agreement on a specific issue by involving as many stakeholders as possible in the decision-making process.

In many companies, managers tend to progressively exclude their employees from decision making as the decisions grow more important. Decisions with the most serious potential impact on the company and its investors are typically made by only a very small group of top managers, operating largely without the input or involvement of workers.

In our experience, the process of consensus building encourages organizations to synthesize original solutions by drawing on the widest possible range of input and information. As long as clearly defined goals, outcomes, and time lines ultimately drive decision making, developing employee consensus around critical business decisions can significantly contribute to the creation of stronger and more vital organizations. Naturally, employees who have been treated like stakeholders and who have participated in decision making are more likely to take responsibility for successful implementation and follow-through.

Consensus building takes time and organizational commitment. As we have seen, in Orpheus our members feel a strong sense of ownership of our musical products and great respect for their colleagues. These qualities form the foundation of our consensus-oriented culture.

In our organization, everyone holds a seat at the decision-making table and has full access to the relevant information. We place a high value on input, and designated leaders throughout our organization constantly solicit it. We also seek to foster trust among all employees and teams, a clear understanding of the problems or opportunities facing the organization, and the willingness to compromise in the interest of achieving the best possible outcomes.

As hierarchies become flatter and organizations increasingly rely on skilled teams and teamwork to make decisions and accomplish goals, the ability to build consensus around company objectives and plans grows ever more important. Consensus encourages the free flow of ideas in a business, while maintaining individual responsibility for product and quality. And, by seeking consensus—and building creative structures that favor consensus—high-performing organizations can implement informed decisions more quickly and effectively.

THE PRINCIPLE

For Orpheus, consensus is an imperative, not an option. Our system of shared and rotating leadership, reliance on informal and formal teams, and emphasis on open communication results in a multitude of opinions that must be weighed and considered as we create our products.

Of course, the search for consensus among dozens of knowledgeable employees, all openly expressing their different perspectives and points of view, could easily degenerate into a time-consuming, frustrating, or unproductive process. We are able to avoid that outcome, because over the years we have developed extremely effective structures for achieving consensus based on team decision making and respectful communication. We also have clear guidelines and well-established mechanisms for breaking the impasses that occasionally and inevitably arise. Our ability to reach consensus quickly and with little employee strife enables us to maintain efficiency in our rehearsal process and gives us an advantage in recruiting the best individuals for positions throughout the organization, thereby strengthening our competitive advantage.

Organizations that seek consensus, and build creative structures that favor consensus, can expect the following benefits:

- Increased worker participation in the decision-making process, leading to better-informed decisions and more invested employees
- Enhanced ability to attract the best employees
- Improved morale and higher employee retention rates

Without practical structures for achieving consensus, companies find it difficult to productively integrate the diverse input of knowledge workers, thereby undermining employee morale, loyalty, and retention. In the sections that follow, you'll see exactly how we at Orpheus and how Sturman

Industries have mastered the art of seeking consensus, and the lessons that can be learned from our examples.

ORPHEUS: A NEED TO BE PRACTICAL

Every company develops its own unique approach to decision making. Some organizations put power in the hands of a few managers, while others, such as ours, involve every employee in the process. In Orpheus, every idea about musical interpretation, repertoire selection, budgets, program design, and strategic planning must be able to attract a critical mass of support from within the organization. Relatively few important matters are unilaterally decided by a single individual; when they are, it is because a consensus has developed to put the decision in that individual's hands. One way or another, a wide range of people have input into all our major decisions, as described in chapter 6.

Our need for consensus is rooted in practical considerations. Like many knowledge workers in today's corporations, our musicians need to be as pragmatic as they are innovative, and each one of our teams has direct responsibility for finding ways to maintain our commercial viability while satisfying our artistic objectives. Ultimately, consensus decision making complements true teamwork by aiming to satisfy the greatest possible number of individuals representing the broadest possible range of constituencies.

It's rare that an organization will reach 100 percent agreement on any issue of consequence. In Orpheus, we have found that achieving a critical mass of opinion is a more realistic and useful objective for our consensus-building efforts, one that helps keep teams focused and individuals cohesive. According to violist Nardo Poy, "You have to be flexible; it's not always going to be your way. There's give and take—you'll give up a little bit this time to get something down the road." Inevitably, consensus requires individuals to compromise, in order to realize organizational objectives.

We designed the Orpheus Process to facilitate consensus building at every level in the organization. Our model resembles an inverted pyramid, building agreement from small permanent or ad hoc teams to progressively larger groups until the entire organization commits to a strategy. The process is extremely flexible; consensus can shift at any time as new information and fresh perspectives are added to the discussion. According to board chairman Gonzalo de Las Heras, "The Orpheus way of building consensus is highly relevant to a decentralized business organization, where you have several decision-making points within a company or group. First, the musicians for each piece agree on a core group, which then argues and comes to a consensus as to what an interpretation should be. Then, they persuade the rest of the group."

Five Assumptions for Agreement

Our ability to consistently achieve consensus on a wide range of matters is largely a function of our fundamental and permanent consensus on five key areas for communication and decision making:

1. **Broad agreement about overall goals and objectives.** Day-to-day disputes focus on how best to achieve objectives, while agreed-upon goals provide coherent standards and criteria for judging possible approaches.
2. **Universal acceptance of the rules of the game.** Orpheus has established complex decision-making processes that are clearly and transparently communicated in job responsibilities and leadership roles. Even when an individual does not completely agree with a decision, he or she respects the authority and responsibility of colleagues or teams to make decisions in appropriate circumstances.
3. **Dependence on open communication.** Designated leaders are charged with soliciting input through formal and informal channels and finding ways to incorporate this feedback before presenting proposed solutions

for decision. Self-managed teams enrich their work with input from outside observers; for example, instrumental sections solicit input from other musicians and core rehearsals incorporate input from the rehearsal coordinator or the artistic directors. And, for every decision, our "marketplace of ideas" environment gives every member the chance to interject his or her ideas and attempt to persuade others to his or her point of view. Decisions, once reached, often reflect and embody many different perspectives. Open communication gives everyone ownership of the decision.

4. **Respect.** A culture of mutual respect ensures broad acceptance of the outcome of decisions because everyone trusts the abilities and motivations of his or her colleagues and the integrity of our decision-making processes.
5. **Experimentation.** The fact that there are few "final" decisions considerably lowers the stakes attached to any particular decision. Controversial decisions are accepted on a trial or experimental basis and members know that they are free, and encouraged, to reopen discussion once there is enough information to evaluate the decision.

Over the years, we have designed a set of structures to enhance our probability of achieving consensus and to provide us with alternatives when consensus is not forthcoming in a reasonable amount of time.

Leading by Consensus

Consensus building is every Orpheus leader's foremost, and sometimes only, responsibility. Most of the time, consensus in our organization arises naturally from fluid two-way communication between leaders and team members; the leader's ideas and vision shape the opinions of others, but are in turn shaped by input they receive from team members. Successful Orpheus leaders usually maintain open communication with individuals and teams throughout the organization, as well as within their own teams; soliciting input and trying out different ideas gives our leaders valuable information, while helping to keep all of our members motivated and engaged.

We do not require consensus from the entire organization for every element of a planned performance, but we do require small-group consensus whenever possible, thereby ensuring that decisions reflect several points of view while avoiding the potential for delay that is inherent in large-scale consensus building. For example, when I finalize the program for a Carnegie Hall concert, I consult closely with the artistic directors but not necessarily with the entire membership of the orchestra. Decisions regarding musical interpretation, on the other hand, belong entirely to the musicians in the orchestra; others in the organization can, and do, offer opinions and ideas, but ultimately the players find consensus among themselves and make the final determinations that shape the performance.

We constantly seek consensus on business matters as well as on artistic questions. For example, we develop our annual operating budget through a six-month collaborative process that involves everyone in the organization, in one way or another. Hundreds of informal conversations and spontaneous meetings involving musicians, administrators, and trustees, as well as the recommendations of numerous ad hoc working groups, go into the development of preliminary proposals by the administrative team. Plans are reviewed and critiqued in formal board committee meetings with musician trustees actively influencing decisions. It's not surprising that by the time our board exercises formal oversight by acting on the proposed budget, consensus is often universal.

Suspending Disbelief for Consensus

Often when we are faced with complex problems, possible solutions will be offered by several different specialists, drawing upon their expertise, and it takes extended deliberation by the project team to determine the best course of action. Achieving consensus under these circumstances usually requires a deep level of honest, open, and patient communication. Often, in the midst of complicated consensus-building discussions, the designated leader or another member of a divided group shifts roles from idea advocate to idea broker. By suspending disbelief, this individual can maintain the integrity of the collaborative process, give every option equal consideration, and (sometimes) creatively combine strategies—all key steps toward fostering consensus.

In September 1999, Orpheus stunned the musical world by bringing the ultimate conductor's signature piece—Beethoven's mighty *Eroica* Symphony—to Carnegie Hall. Performing the symphony was tantamount to launching a new and enormously complex product line, and the rehearsals for this monumental work were especially challenging. Profound differences of approach that first emerged within the leadership core quickly spilled over into the full orchestra and, after the first full rehearsal, two radically different artistic approaches quickly emerged, one represented by the concertmaster, Todd Phillips, and one by the principal second violin, Guillermo Figueroa. (Both were members of the leadership core for this project.) Phillips supported a broader, weightier approach to the music while Figueroa urged a much faster, livelier interpretation. As the rehearsals progressed and numerous incarnations of both concepts were discussed and tried, it became apparent that the orchestra was deeply divided on a matter of fundamental importance. A vote was taken, and the group split 50/50.

The issue continued unresolved all the way to the dress rehearsal at Carnegie Hall, when Ronnie Bauch (who was rehearsal coordinator for this concert) asked Figueroa to serve as an idea broker, listening from the audience as Phillips led the group in his approach. Figueroa did so, and reported back that while he personally continued to support his own approach, he had a suggestion that might make Phillips's interpretation work more successfully: exaggerating the phrasing to create forward momentum as well as weight. Suddenly, musicians who moments earlier had been in opposite interpretive camps were excitedly voicing ideas about how to synthesize the best elements of both approaches to the music, and Phillips was reshaping his approach to find more ways to keep up the music's driving motion. The synthesis satisfied most of the orchestra, and the outcome proved to be a critical and popular success. Assigning the responsibility of being an idea broker to a member of a decision-making team consistently helps us achieve consensus in artistic and administrative areas.

Facilitating a Solution

Sometimes, it takes an idea broker from outside of the immediate project team to help us to facilitate solutions that reach consensus. For example, in April 1999 Orpheus premiered an orchestral version of Beethoven's Quartet no. 14, op. 131—forty-five minutes of technically, intellectually, and emotionally challenging music, played without pause. For the Carnegie Hall premiere, the orchestra urgently needed a designated listener to give input on dozens of unresolved questions, but none of the performers felt they could afford to leave the stage because the issues were so subtle that the absence of a single musician would disrupt the overall balance. Each section leader wanted members of another section to do the listening, and none were willing to let their own members go.

Finally, Orpheus violinist Eric Wyrick, who was not playing in this particular concert, volunteered to come to the dress rehearsal to listen and make suggestions. All the section leaders agreed to work with him as a designated listener. In rehearsal, a sharp disagreement arose between violinist Guillermo Figueroa and cellist Melissa Meell (both members of the leadership core) over the balance of sound between their respective sections. Both agreed that if the cellos and first violins played at the same volume, the blend of the ensemble would be affected negatively, but Figueroa thought the cellos should play softer, while Meell thought the first violins should. The entire orchestra was also split, so the group tried both ideas. Neither one achieved a satisfying result.

Serving as the designated listener, Wyrick suggested that the cellos turn their chairs and instruments toward the audience to give them more presence in the overall sound, allowing them to be heard clearly but without the "heaviness" everyone was trying to avoid. The orchestra agreed to try this new seating configuration, and both the cello and violin sections agreed to play softer. The result, enthusiastically embraced by the entire orchestra, allowed for both successful projection and balanced instrumental blend. Wyrick's outside perspective was backed by his own expertise, a grant of authority as the idea broker, and the openness of the orchestra to share decision making with someone outside of the performance group or smaller teams.

When Consensus Fails

Even with a commitment to and guidelines for reaching consensus, we do not always succeed. Continuing to seek consensus after it becomes clear that none will be achieved can impair the effectiveness of the team to work through other matters, and ultimately affect the entire organization. What happens when consensus can't be reached? Sometimes, when time is of the essence, especially under performance conditions, designated leaders make the choices. However, if time and circumstance permit, the group takes a vote to decide the issue.

To the greatest extent possible, we resolve issues at the level where people are most directly affected by the outcome; this means that all purely artistic matters (that is, matters that do not impact the orchestra's image, marketability, or external relations) are directly in the hands of the musicians. Although the musicians, through their leadership structures and team approach, make thousands of decisions every year concerning personnel, seating, and interpretation, only *two or three issues each year* are actually resolved by vote. In the early days of Orpheus, the full orchestra voted on dozens of matters in what was a much shorter season. A decade ago, the average was eight to ten votes per year. Our declining reliance on voting to break deadlocks can be traced to four principles that have emerged over the years, and that are now at the heart of our decision-making process:

1. We have established a clear standard of quality that is universally shared among our members and teams.
2. We have developed a well-structured and practiced team approach to leadership, increasing members' willingness to rely on designated leaders to resolve differences that require decisions in a tight time frame.
3. We have increased the number of decisions we delegate to the "local," smaller group level (that is, among the winds, strings, core groups, and so forth), much as we have placed more general decision-making authority in the hands of the people doing the work.
4. Leadership teams solicit input from outside the team, before arriving at difficult or controversial decisions that will inevitably impact the entire orchestra.

Only if teams at the "local levels" remain at an impasse, after seeking input from other members outside the small group, do matters move up to a larger team for resolution. So, although there are only two or three orchestral votes each year, there may be ten times as many votes in the viola section.

Designating methods for conflict resolution when consensus doesn't emerge helps to speed consensus building in other decisions. Teams are often empowered to resolve disputes themselves, working through the range of possibilities defined by our strategic objectives, mission, and operational needs.

It helps enormously that few decisions in Orpheus are truly "permanent." In our continuing effort to perfect our musical products, the choices made for one night's concert are carefully scrutinized and often revisited the next morning. The same is true of operating plans and boardroom resolutions. Says Ronnie Bauch, "There is no one way to do anything, so although we reach consensus, the decision may last for only one performance. Afterward, we may say, 'Well, that was interesting, but let's try it another way.' There's a group consciousness when something doesn't work. What's interesting is that often the person who advanced an idea says, 'You know, that really didn't work.' That's an important part of what makes the group so successful."

This means that, ultimately, consensus in Orpheus is rarely static. As flutist Susan Palma-Nidel points out, "At a certain point, you have to go out and play, so you have to agree to agree. But that doesn't necessarily mean that people are giving up on their ideas. Sometimes, when we are out there playing and we've done the piece a couple of times, aspects we were never able to agree about suddenly make sense. You have to leave open the possibility of change and continued discussion, because that's how we grow. If we get too settled in on the ideal of consensus, we risk sounding too flattened out and even. That's a very real danger."

STURMAN: BUILDING CONSENSUS ONE PERSON AT A TIME

While some company owners and CEOs make the majority of their organizations' important decisions, often cutting lower-level employees out of the process, some managers use consensus as an effective tool for making decisions, even in industries that seem to depend on command-and-control for survival. These managers recognize that obtaining consensus among all employees in an organization results in better ideas and a greater sense of employee ownership, both of which directly benefit the company, its employees, and its customers.

At Sturman Industries, a 170-person designer and manufacturer of digital valves in Woodland Park, Colorado, only one employee has a job title: the president and cofounder, Carol Sturman. Every other person working for the company, which makes products used for a variety of automotive, beverage dispensing, and irrigation applications, is identified only by the name of the team to which they are assigned. Sturman's hierarchy is flat, and employees are assigned to self-managing teams.

Founded in 1989, Sturman Industries aims to change the world with its unique technology and its approach to doing business. On the technology side, Sturman found its niche with magnetically latching, electronically controlled valves that cofounder Eddie Sturman originally invented for NASA's Apollo space program; these smaller, faster, and more efficient valves became a breakthrough for the automotive industry. Today, Sturman—in a joint venture with International Truck and Engine Company, the world's largest producer of midsized diesel engines—is developing a more efficient diesel fuel injector that will pollute less and be more fuel efficient than existing designs.

A Culture for Changing the World

On the business side, Sturman has made a conscious decision to take a road less traveled by creating a special working environment for employees. The company's culture is informal and relaxed. Employees hold substantial responsibility and, more important, the authority they need to get things done. The company's sixty-two-thousand-square-foot home office—situated on six hundred acres of partially forested, rolling hills with a view of Colorado's Pike's Peak—looks and feels quite different from the headquarters of most industrial firms. Walk across a covered wooden bridge and enter Sturman's front doors, and you'll find yourself in a large, comfortable lobby dominated by a massive stone fireplace and furnished with leather sofas. Oriental carpets cover wooden floors, vaulted wooden-beam ceilings complement an open floor plan, machine shops have picture windows offering breathtaking mountain views, voice and data ports are situated on outdoor decks overlooking the mountains, and there's a pool table located on the second floor.

Even as the company has grown dramatically, Carol and Eddie Sturman remain committed to keeping alive the small-family spirit that has been a part of Sturman's culture since its founding. Says Carol Sturman, "When we designed our current building, I struggled with traditional office design versus the way we organized ourselves when we were a friendly, small company; I was afraid that we would lose the special environment we had. I told the architect, 'I don't want it to look like an office or a manufacturing building. I want it to look like a high-tech lodge.'"

Two Organizational Systems

Sturman uses two major overlapping systems to organize its workforce and activities. For external communication purposes, every employee belongs to a functional group, such as administration, electrical engineering, production, or quality, which helps identify employees to customers and vendors. But, for internal purposes, the company organizes into project teams, and employees can participate in more than one of these functional groups at the same time.

Each group has a coordinator who ensures that its administrative needs are met, and a leader who coordinates goals and products, but team structure is employed with flexibility, leaving team members with a great deal of room for freedom and experimentation. One group, for example, has a technical coordinator and an administrative coordinator, and some groups have decided to rotate the coordinator role among different members of the team. According to Nancy Ochsner of Sturman's People to People department, "As [we] started growing, and we started breaking out into functional groups, some people naturally took on leadership roles. Some groups would rotate the coordinator position and other groups installed one person to do the job. Our goal was to allow every group to be able to make their own decisions—not have someone make them for them—build more consensus."

Functional groups meet at least once a month, and the coordinators from each functional group meet together once a month as well. Anyone in the company can raise any issue during functional group meetings and, if the group believes that the issue under discussion needs to be addressed by the whole company, then the group's coordinator will bring it up at the monthly coordinators' meeting where the issue will be discussed.

Allowing each group to determine how leadership is designated and how decisions are made gives employees a stake in participating and increases the chance that consensus will be reached. Says Marc Andrew Wolverton, an employee in the Production Development group, "Our coordinator is more of a facilitator, and meetings are mostly informational. To get everybody on the same page when something needs to be decided, our facilitator will invite all of our opinions, and a decision is made by group consensus." Just as important, however, employees know coordinators will step in to make decisions if the team fails to reach consensus.

A Commitment to Consensus

The commitment to consensus, and the practice of involving all employees in the decision-making process on matters ranging from customer deadlines to long-term goals and values, unlocks the creativity and talent within every employee and ultimately leads to better decisions. Says Carol Sturman, "I think what this company does is get the best out of everybody. Most companies don't tap into the highest potential of each person. We encourage people to seek us out, and to give feedback to their teams. What do you think? How can we improve? How can we be better? We have a lot of different communication avenues for that."

Sturman's process for designing and implementing a drug-free workplace program clearly illustrates its commitment to consensus. In most companies, drug policy is not open to discussion by the entire workforce; it is simply enacted and enforced. Sturman approached the subject differently. Says Nancy Ochsner, "The first question was, 'Is this something that we want to do at this point? Our employee assistance program [EAP] had asked if we wanted to be part of a grant they offer for developing drug-free workplaces in small companies, so we talked about it. We pulled all the research. It was a good time to consider a drug-free workplace policy, and involving employees would ensure that we address drug abuse in a humane way and with a policy in place."

Although the company's EAP wanted them to initiate a comprehensive program of prehire and random testing, Sturman believes such testing contradicts its workplace culture. Because the company focuses its attention on how employees perform on the job, Sturman's leadership team decided that testing would only be conducted after accidents and for probable cause.

Very early in the process, Sturman brought its coordinators together and showed them a fairly vague draft policy. That started a firestorm of debate within the company, but employees were most opposed to the policy's cold and impersonal language, not the rules it outlined. After soliciting and listening to everyone's opinions, Sturman revised the draft to make it more respectful, by emphasizing the company's desire to make working conditions safe for everyone and providing an avenue for employees to find help with drug abuse problems if needed. The revised policy was again presented to the company's coordinators for discussion, and they unanimously approved it. Though there's no doubt that imposing a drug-free workplace policy on employees without seeking their input or suggestions would be a much more expedient way to do business, building consensus on the decision strengthened employee commitment to the policy—and to the company—in the long run.

Sturman faced a similar challenge when Colorado law required the company to notify employees that it is an "at-will" employer, where employees can be fired at any time for any reason. Developing consensus on how to communicate the policy allowed Sturman to underscore that employees were valued rather than expendable. According to Nancy Ochsner, "They were insulted. But they were right. So I went to several attorneys and found a way to write the policy that is reasonable without offending people."

While some companies ask their employees for limited input in goal setting, most often employees have no role at all, because managers and executives set goals and employees meet them. Sturman Industries takes an approach that involves the entire company in setting company goals and determining what objectives will be addressed. According to Carol Sturman,

"Setting our annual goals is an activity that involves the entire company. One month, we get everyone together to talk about what our focus should be for that year. The next month we'll divide into mixed teams to address the specific categories that we said we should focus on. Then we decide what we think the priorities should be for the whole company for that year. Employees aren't just thinking about their own little group; they're thinking about the whole company. The teams put their own ideas in along with the ideas from the rest of the company, then they pick out the goals that relate specifically to them, and then they announce their two or three goals for each category for the year."

Building consensus isn't an easy process, even in an organization that has a culture deeply rooted in it. Every employee is unique, and different employees bring different skills and experiences to the table. According to Ochsner, "The interesting thing you find in a place like this is that people are different. [Our main business] is research and development, so they're pretty open and free thinkers, but production isn't. You bring in people, for example, who've been machinists for years, and they're used to being told what to do. We found that it put a lot of stress on many of them to ask their opinion and to encourage them to come to us with solutions; it just didn't work for everybody. One man said 'Isn't that what you guys were hired to do?' But, despite the occasional discomfort, more often than not, people like being asked and being able to have a voice." Says Production Development group employee Marc Andrew Wolverton, "Bring the team into the decision-making process and give them ownership of the program."

PUTTING THIS PRINCIPLE INTO PRACTICE

In companies with heavy hierarchies and autocratic leaders, consensus is neither necessary nor expected in implementing decisions. Consensus is essential, however, to making decisions and meeting goals in team-based organizations. When implementing a decision affects a large number of employees, and carries a great opportunity or risk for a company, developing consensus becomes imperative.

Five Steps for Using Consensus Decision Making

STEP 1: **Have a plan to reach consensus.** For many organizations—especially those that have long operated under hierarchical decision-making systems that concentrate authority in the hands of a few managers—consensus building does not come naturally or easily. Every organization can benefit by having a plan for reaching consensus; here are some key components:

a. Define the problem or decision to be reached.
b. Agree on the objectives and goals for the issue being discussed.
c. Brainstorm as many alternative approaches as possible.
d. Narrow down the list of possible approaches to a manageable number (ten or less), using votes if necessary.
e. Discuss the pros and cons of each remaining approach; adjust and compromise as required to satisfy people's needs.
f. Decide on the best approach.
g. If consensus isn't reached, look at areas of disagreement and work to resolve them. Repeat steps e and f.
h. When consensus is reached, act on it.

STEP 2: **Solicit "what if" proposals from all employees (and then seriously consider them).** Former chairman and CEO of Sony Pictures Entertainment, and current chairman of Culver City, California–based Mandalay Entertainment Peter Guber tells the story of how an inexperienced member of a film crew solved a difficult and potentially costly production problem: how to get gorillas to act for the camera: "We called an emergency meeting to solve these problems. In the middle of it, a young intern asked, 'What if you let the gorillas write the story?' Everyone laughed and wondered what she was doing in a meeting with experienced filmmakers. Hours later, someone casually asked her what she had meant. She said, 'What if you sent a really good cinematographer into the jungle with a ton of film to shoot the gorillas? Then you could write a story around what the gorillas did on film.' It was a brilliant idea. And we did exactly what she suggested—we sent Alan Root, an Academy Award–nominated cinematographer, into the jungle for three weeks. He came back with phenomenal footage that practically wrote the story for us. We shot the film for $20 million—half of the original budget! This woman's 'inexperience' enabled her to see opportunities where we saw only boundaries. This experience taught me three things. First, ask high-quality questions, like 'What if?' Second, find people who add new perspectives and create new conversations. As experienced filmmakers, we believed that our way was the only way—and that the intern lacked the experience to have an opinion. Third, pay attention to those new voices. If you want unlimited options for solving a problem, engage the 'what if' before you lock onto the how to. You'll be surprised by what you discover."[1]

STEP 3: Work to resolve differences between employee points of view. As anyone in business knows, trying to reach consensus within a group of vocal, self-confident, and assertive people can be a difficult task. At General Electric's Durham, North Carolina, aircraft engine assembly plant, consensus isn't left to chance. Employees receive extensive training in how to reach consensus; in fact, the company invests about $500 million annually on training and education programs on a variety of topics, including consensus building, for employees at all levels.[2] According to technician Duane Williams, "Everybody doesn't see things in the same way. But we've had training on how to reach consensus. We've had training on how to live with ideas that we might not necessarily agree with. All the things you normally fuss and moan about to yourself and your buddies—well, we have a chance to do something about them. I can't say, 'They' don't know what's going on, or, 'They' made a bad decision. I am 'they.' "[3]

STEP 4: Encourage managers to look to employees for solutions. It can be difficult for some managers to step back from the decision-making process and let others in the organization participate, especially when time is of the essence. Most managers pride themselves on their ability to make quick decisions, so they often default to their own ideas rather than take the extra time or effort to involve all employees. But, according to Jeffrey Swartz, president and CEO of shoemaker Timberland Company of Stratham, New Hampshire, companies reach their best decisions when everyone plays a part in developing solutions. Says Swartz, "As a leader, one of the biggest things I've learned is that I don't always have to be right. I used to feel that the only way to justify my egregious salary was to tell people what to do. I don't let myself do that anymore. Instead, I leave people alone and trust that they'll come up with a suitable solution—and, in turn, that process perpetuates a learning environment. For instance, we've been trying to create a day-care program at Timberland. Several years ago, I commissioned outside people to design a program. They came back with a model that no one wanted. But at a company rally recently, a woman asked me what I was going to do about day care. I told her that I was not going to do anything about it. My kids are getting older, and they don't need day care. The place went silent. But then I said that if she needs day care and if it's relevant for the company, then she should let me know what she wants to do about it. So what did she do? She organized a group that polled other employees, researched the cost of a day-care program, and identified where the funding would come from. Then she held a meeting to present the group's case to me. When I asked her why she had invited me to the meeting, she said, 'To applaud.' That meeting was spectacular! The group still has some issues to work out before the program is implemented, but the way the group tackled the problem was amazing. All I did was move out of the way."[4]

Step 5: Practice building consensus. For an organization not used to working toward consensus, practicing the process can help build organizational muscles for making consensus work. Here is an exercise to help teach consensus-building skills to employees:

a. Have employees pair up. Select a particularly controversial work-related issue for each pair to discuss, such as the company's drug-testing policies or its pay structure.

b. Direct each member of the pair to express his or her opinion on the issue for three minutes.
c. Ask the members of each pair of employees to make a concerted effort to come up with a consensus position that both members can agree to. Have them put this position in writing.
d. Merge the pairs to form new groups of four members each. Have someone from each of the original pairs read their consensus position to the other pair. Ask the members to work together to merge their positions to develop a new consensus opinion that all four members of the new groups can agree to.
e. Repeat this process while creating ever-larger groups, first members of eight, then sixteen, and so forth until all employees are in one group. When this final group is able to reach a consensus position, have the group write it down and post it on the wall. The group has reached consensus.

Potential Traps and Land Mines

- **Mistaking one dominant voice for consensus.** Oversize egos can become a destructive force in any organization. Successful organizations draw knowledge, confidence, and strength from diverse employee personalities, points of view, and experiences—provided that these are carefully balanced. Focus on building consensus out of creative disagreement and give everyone an equal voice in the process. When one person dominates decisions or forces employees to support an idea, take immediate action by:
  - Talking to the employee and explaining the damage that he or she is doing to the organization and to his or her coworkers.
  - Describing and encouraging the kind of behavior you want to see.
  - Rewarding consensus-building behavior over unilateral decision making.

- **People spending too much time talking and not enough time listening.** True consensus cannot be reached in an organization where employees talk but few people listen. In your own communication, be sure that you spend at least as much time listening to what your employees and coworkers have to say as you spend talking. You can encourage others to listen by pursuing the following steps:
  - **Ask questions.** Asking questions of many employees, and asking their colleagues to incorporate others' ideas into their own, requires listening. By asking questions that probe into an issue in a non-threatening and supportive way, you'll draw out listeners and help build a foundation for consensus.
  - **Express your interest.** If you show interest in another person's opinion, especially someone who is shy in giving it, you'll greatly increase the likelihood that others will pay attention as well. Avoid yawning, interrupting conversations to take phone calls, and similar behaviors that indicate a lack of interest.
  - **Take notes.** By taking notes, you demonstrate a clear interest in and commitment to hearing each speaker and help the group see and organize a range of ideas.
- **Lack of clear organizational mission.** If an organization doesn't have a clear mission, no one can definitively state its goals, much less whether or not the search for consensus on a particular issue has resulted in the best outcome for the organization. A mission gives all decision making a sense of purpose. Without a clear and compelling mission, most companies will find it difficult to reach consensus on a huge range of critical tasks, from allocating resources to targeting customers and inspiring employees. Conversely, companies with a clear mission often enjoy the advantage of a united and engaged workforce; consensus comes more easily among employees who have a shared sense of purpose and view one another as allies rather than threats.

Motivating employees, earning their loyalty, and encouraging their best performance require giving them a stake in the business by fully involving them in a company's strategic decisions. In the short run building consensus is more time consuming and labor-intensive than simply giving orders, but over time companies who do so will see large gains in employee performance and project success. Although both Orpheus and Sturman Industries recognize that there are times when decisions have to be made and actions taken, whether or not consensus has been reached, each organization takes active steps to nurture a culture where those situations are the exception and not the rule.

9

Dedicate Passionately to Your Mission

Motivation will almost always beat mere talent.

—NORMAN AUGUSTINE, FORMER PRESIDENT AND CEO, MARTIN LOCKHEED

It was the Scottish historian Thomas Carlyle who said, "Music is well said to be the speech of angels; in fact, nothing among the utterances allowed to man is felt to be so divine. It brings us near to the Infinite." Music has a unique ability to transcend words and speak directly, on an intuitive level, to the full range of human emotions and aspirations. A great orchestra performing at its best fills the air with electricity, quickening the pulse and uplifting the soul. Music has the power to unite, inspire, and even on occasion to change the course of history.

But, what is it that separates truly great performances from those that are merely good? What is it that can make one group of people—whether an orchestra or a business—appear uninspired and lackadaisical about their work, while another group seems energized, internally motivated, and ready to do whatever it takes to meet the challenges of excellence? It's passion, a drive to achieve performance that approaches perfection itself.

In the 1940s, psychologist Abraham Maslow developed his famous hierarchy of human motivation, a pyramid of human needs. At the base of the motivational pyramid are the fundamental physiological necessities such as food, water, and shelter, while at the very top—above security, social interaction, and even esteem—is the need for "self-actualization." Translating Maslow's pyramid to the workplace, the higher a job rises in the hierarchy, the greater the motivation of the individual performing it to excel. Salary and benefits give employees the means to attain their basic needs, a safe working environment provides security; teamwork fosters social interaction; and shared responsibility for creating a quality product builds individual esteem.

When self-actualization, the most powerful motivational force in Maslow's hierarchy, is unleashed in the workplace, individuals tend to experience work as their own personal and uniquely valuable contribution to the world around them. Employees who view their jobs as opportunities to express their highest selves—to become "the best they can be"—strive passionately to achieve the extraordinary as a matter of routine, every day. Not surprisingly, organizations that foster and constructively channel passion in their workers create environments that produce remarkable levels of accomplishment.

Orpheus sets exceptionally high standards; in our culture, yesterday's triumph inevitably provokes discussion and analysis. New choices, designed to make tomorrow's performance even better, are constantly under consideration. We do this because we are all passionately dedicated to accomplishing our mission, and so, in a deep and personal sense, our organization's outcomes matter a great deal to each individual. The success of our model of collaborative management proves more than just the advantages of sharing and rotating leadership, investing individuals with a full stake in the organization's decision making, putting power and responsibility in the hands of the people doing the work, and so on. It demonstrates the extraordinary power of passionate dedication to motivate individuals and organizations to excel.

For an organization to fully realize the benefits of collaborative management, its members need a shared mission they can dedicate themselves to, and the organization needs to find employees who are passionately motivated by the mission to personally create the best products possible. The Orpheus Process is built on individual motivation, capturing the passionate dedication of our musicians to music making and channeling it into the highest possible level of organizational performance.

Cellist Eric Bartlett describes one particularly memorable Orpheus performance in the fabled Musikverein, home of the Vienna Philharmonic, that still inspires him more than fifteen years later: "From the moment we went out, we were at our peak and completely dedicated to performing our best. We truly gave it our all, and, to our surprise, the knowledgeable and jaded Viennese public went *nuts*. They gave us four curtain calls for the first piece in our program, which never happens. With the first piece on the program your goal is to wake them up. They understood that an Orpheus concert is a relationship between the audience and the musicians."

Achieving that level of performance is the fundamental objective of the Orpheus Process. We succeed because everyone in our organization is highly motivated—indeed, passionate—about doing so.

THE PRINCIPLE

Passionate employees make a bottom-line difference; without them, even the best-trained, well-equipped, and generously funded companies find it difficult to excel in the long run. A shared sense of purpose can unite a diverse workforce and motivate it to extraordinary levels of excellence, under even the most difficult conditions. When knowledge workers, in particular, can see—and are recognized for—their personal imprints on their organization's products and success, they perform at their highest levels.

To take full advantage of collaborative management, an organization must deeply engage its employees in its processes and personally invest them in its outcomes. On the other hand, organizations that rely on punishment, fear, coercion, and intimidation to motivate employees are doomed to significant competitive disadvantage. In the words of management guru Tom Peters, "If you're working in a company that is not enthusiastic, energetic, creative, clever, curious, and just plain fun, you've got troubles, serious troubles."[1]

In the pages that follow, you'll get a close look at how we identify and inspire passion in our members, and how a passion for mission brings out the best in the individuals who work for socially conscious yogurt-maker Stonyfield Farm.

ORPHEUS: A REAL PASSION FOR THE MUSIC

Orpheus has a clear mission: to bring the collaborative and cooperative principles of chamber music to orchestral performance in order to provide the public with musical experiences of the highest artistic quality. The chamber music model, with its focus on respect and trust, provided us with the means to define our mission in terms of each member's contribution to superior performance. Yet, we must continually find new ways to use our mission to inspire the highest degree of motivation from every individual in our organization.

Where does passionate dedication come from?

For us, passionate dedication begins with the music itself. According to violinist Ronnie Bauch, "Passion for music drives Orpheus. If the members felt that having a conductor would bring the finest level of expression and interpretation, then they would hire a conductor." Orpheus's dedication to "finding the chamber music heart of orchestral repertoire" led our founding members to give unprecedented authority to the members who were already very dedicated to the music itself. The combination set in motion a unique culture that, nearly thirty years later, still finds new ways to channel the passion of many individuals into the collaborative creation of a consistently superior product.

In effect, our mission allows us to place self-actualization at the very center of our business plan. To do so, we encourage each individual to bring passion into every performance; doing so heightens each person's trust in one another, the organization, and its mission. In Orpheus, passion holds our organization together, unites our members, and compels us to work in consensus-building teams for a common purpose. It also helps us recruit and retain talented employees even when we cannot match a competitor's material compensation.

Building a Mission-Driven Company

Our mission permits—and requires—each member to accept personal responsibility for each of the key elements of our product: the quality of the musical performance; the value of working collaboratively to create a product of beauty and power; and the importance of educating and engaging new audiences. In Orpheus, passion motivates individuals to undertake challenging and ambitious responsibilities. We reinforce individual passion by using our mission to shape our tactical and strategic decision making. Everyone in Orpheus knows that our mission is more than a poster nailed to the wall.

We believe that any company can begin the process of tying its strategic objectives and goals to its mission and use this process to enhance employee motivation. While Orpheus's fundamental mission has not changed since 1972, our strategic objectives and goals continually evolve from the ground up, based on the input of orchestra members, trustees, and administrators. Although classical music is a field more noted for respecting tradition than for openness to change, we have consistently used our mission to expand audiences and develop new products, including revenue-generating management seminars.

Each of the separate principles of the Orpheus Process help us keep employees passionate about their work, and each member of Orpheus knows that his or her talents and abilities make a unique and irreplaceable contribution to our mission. Without passionate members, we would require a conductor to set the standards of performance and motivate individuals as best as possible to meet that standard. When employees lack internal motivation for their work, businesses often turn to an authority figure to improve job performance, but at an enormous cost to the creativity and productivity of the entire workforce.

Competition and Company Mission

A strong sense of corporate mission can give a company a substantial competitive advantage, creating a basis for strategic focus while building employee motivation and consumer loyalty. The evolution of our mission during the late 1990s is a case in point.

In 1998, alarmed by the drop in our revenues and the global decline in classical music audiences that spread from the United States to Europe and Asia, we conducted market research to determine where consumers were going and how we could regain them. The research uncovered an unexpected finding: intelligent, sophisticated, and adventurous culture consumers—the same people who go to museums, adult-education programs, plays, and dance concerts—thought that they were "too dumb" to understand and appreciate classical music. Specifically, these people were afraid that they wouldn't know how to pronounce names, what to say at intermission, or when to applaud. Fear of making faux pas scared away the very customers most likely to consume, and enjoy, our product. Fortunately, our research also showed that our unique way of performing orchestral music without a conductor, and the values of teamwork and collaboration we celebrate in our performances, held immense appeal to this large untapped market.

Our response to this information was to set out immediately to use our mission as a resource to help us overcome the barriers that were holding us back in the marketplace. Our first step was to begin to rearticulate our mission to engage the public. Formal and informal teams throughout the organization focused on designing and funding new programs and reshaping the concert experience to make our performances more "user friendly."

The results were rapid—and dramatic. In just two years, we reversed the revenue drop, created new educational programs and repertoire to develop young audiences, launched university residencies featuring the orchestra and its music, and raised millions of dollars to support these new programs. At the same time, we expanded our broadcast, recording, and new media activities, reaching millions of new customers around the world, and highlighted the orchestra's mission in concerts and promotions.

Often companies will make the mistake of confusing their advertising slogans with an organizational mission, or vice versa. Our experience proves that a mission can help an organization develop new projects and even a unique identity in an industry, if it also allows employees to develop their own passions and expertise. Today, our work goes far beyond the province of typical orchestras to include leadership seminars for businesses and conflict resolution training in the nonprofit sector. These radical initiatives were proposed and realized by our members, who were motivated by their passionate dedication to our mission and spurred by the challenge of expanding our audience.

Practicing Passion

Our way of working is labor-intensive. Onstage and off, the Orpheus Process takes a great deal of effort, and each one of us must constantly practice and remaster our roles to keep the organization moving to new heights of excellence. Board member Jerry Gladstein, who has watched the orchestra perform for years, captures the way passion transforms Orpheus: "They get great gratification out of performing very well. When there's an exceptional performance, everybody knows it. I still remember one night in London about ten years ago, when the legendary Alfred Brendel joined the group as soloist. I went backstage, and half of the people were in tears. And Brendel said to me, 'Man, I thought we were going to fly away. I thought we were going to fly away.' "

How do we foster passionate dedication to our mission, year after year? In our experience, the most powerful motivation comes from *within* individuals. Therefore, the most direct and effective way we sustain a passionate level of dedication throughout our organization is to recruit and hire people who already care deeply about our mission. In my years at Orpheus, I have found that there are two other things that make a significant difference. The first is maintaining a working environment that encourages each person to translate his or her individual passion into a personal contribution to the organization's commitment to excellence and rewards such behavior. The second is—whenever possible—keeping managers out of the way, so as to avoid coming between individuals and their own powerful motivation to excel.

STONYFIELD FARM: OUT TO CHANGE THE WORLD

Most, if not all, companies are started with the flame of an entrepreneurial founder's passion and vision. Over time, as these companies mature and institutionalize, keeping the flame alive—and the motivation for high performance that comes with it—can become increasingly difficult. As a result, growing organizations are constantly faced with the strategic challenge of maintaining consistent missions while continuing to inspire their employees.

Londonderry, New Hampshire–based Stonyfield Farm is a company that has creatively and effectively responded to the challenge of sustaining passionate dedication among its workers through years of growth and evolution. From its origins as a not-for-profit organic farming project, Stonyfield Farm has rapidly grown into a thriving for-profit commercial enterprise with annual sales of more than $60 million; the company is currently the fourth-largest yogurt producer in the United States. The keys to Stonyfield Farm's ability to successfully mobilize its workforce to accomplish this extraordinary transformation have been employee-based strategic planning and a unique bottom line–oriented approach to accomplishing the company's mission that couples passion with profit.

Leading with Their Mission

Throughout its history, Stonyfield Farm's success story has been intertwined with a mission-first attitude that drives the company's decisions, inspiring employees and building loyalty among the company's stakeholders. Stonyfield Farm first committed to its mission long before it developed any kind of business plan. In fact, the company went into the yogurt business to raise money to support an organic farming school. Gary Hirshberg, who served as one of the school's volunteer trustees and is now Stonyfield's president and CEO, describes the importance of mission to the history of his company: "It's a story built on the hypothesis that we could lead with our mission, and the rest would work out. And I'm pleased to say we've proven it. Not only has having this mission been a competitive advantage, but it's gotten us through hard times and been incredibly important for employee and consumer loyalty and retention."

Stonyfield's mission statement starts by providing employees with a clear and compelling standard for high quality: "To produce the very highest quality all natural and certified organic products." The statement also encompasses objectives that purposefully aim to motivate the company's key constituencies:

- **Employees.** "To provide a healthful, productive, and enjoyable workplace for all employees, with opportunities to gain new skills and advance personal career goals."
- **Consumers and vendors:** "To educate consumers and producers about the value of protecting the environment and of supporting family farmers and sustainable farming methods."
- **Investors and lenders:** "To serve as a model that environmentally and socially responsible businesses can also be profitable" and "to recognize our obligation to stockholders and lenders by providing an excellent return on their investment."

Today, Stonyfield keeps its founding mission current by setting aside 10 percent of its pretax profits for environmental groups, recycling 70 percent of the waste produced in its yogurt plants, and planting trees to compensate for ozone-harming carbon emissions. The company also keeps its mission front and center with customers through marketing and educational campaigns like the well-known Stonyfield Lid Program, which highlights opportunities for environmental action with consumer-oriented slogans like "Make Your Voice 'Cow'nt' for Organic Standards" printed every four to six weeks on 1.75 million yogurt container lids.

But the bottom line of the company's mission is quality. Stonyfield utilizes a quirky, socially active attitude to motivate employees and target environmentally aware customers, but every employee at the company realizes that being an environmentally aware company is not enough to beat out competition. Consumers must also get a high-quality product that matches and exceeds other manufacturers'.

Motivation and Mission

In the years since its founding as a fund-raising project for a not-for-profit organic farm, Stonyfield has undergone radical change in size, scope of operations, and employee skills. Most significantly, it shifted from a not-for-profit (that is, operated as a trust for the public benefit) to a for-profit (that is, operated as a commercial enterprise for the benefit of shareholders) company. By the mid-1990s, an organization that seemed by definition to be based on its members' collective passion for their mission needed a new road map to help it compete successfully in the for-profit world.

At a staff retreat in 1996, Stonyfield Farm gave a team of its employees free rein to envision a new strategic plan, based on their personal passion for a vital element of the company's mission—to operate as an environmentally sustainable company. The result was the employee-initiated *Stonyfield Farm Environmental Cookbook,* a long-term strategy for creating a business that gives more to the planet than it takes away while creating profits for shareholders. The *Stonyfield Farm Environmental Cookbook* functions primarily as a working blueprint, helping to encourage (and focus) employee initiatives that contribute to a model of sustainability. Stonyfield's employees have responded in many creative and effective ways, often with significant impact—in large part because the company constantly gives them the opportunity to initiate projects that reflect their own passion for the mission, as long at these projects also advance the strategic objectives of Stonyfield's business plan.

For example, in 1996 a group of Stonyfield employees decided to try to find ways to offset the amount of the "greenhouse effect"—producing carbon dioxide gas (CO_2) that the company's operations were producing. The team calculated that by reinvesting some of the savings generated by the company's various energy reduction programs in tree planting, they could transform Stonyfield into a zero-emissions company by 2002. In 1997, five years ahead of schedule, Stonyfield succeeded in meeting its goal by heavily investing in a reforestation project in Oregon—an initiative that will save the company money in the long term and therefore increased shareholder value.

More recently, Stonyfield's research revealed that as their market share grew, increasing numbers of their consumers needed reasons to motivate or reinforce the choice of an expensive Stonyfield product over a less costly nonorganic competitor. Furthermore, market research indicated that many customers were simply confused about what made a product "organic." A team of Stonyfield employees responded by drafting *A Practical Guide to Understanding Organic*, a guide to organic product truths and falsehoods that was designed to educate consumers about the advantages of organic products. In addition to giving the public better information, the guide had the unanticipated benefit of reawakening employee passion for Stonyfield's mission. Organic products impose extra burdens on employees (special paperwork and certifications) as well as consumers (higher prices). As consumer demand for Stonyfield's products increased, employees felt the pressure; the guide helped employees translate their passion for the company's mission into motivation for coping with increased day-to-day workplace challenges.

Personal Passion

To maintain staff levels in a tight labor market, Stonyfield makes a point of hiring for skills; thus belief in the company's mission is not a criterion for hiring new employees. Instead, the company prefers to recruit individuals with high levels of professional motivation or expertise, relying on being able to find subsequent ways to connect their employees to the mission after they join the organization. This requires that Stonyfield undertake a substantial and ongoing education effort. It isn't easy to get new employees to internalize a company's mission—even in a company like Stonyfield, which thoroughly integrates its mission into its business plans and practices.

To tap into their employees' personal passions, Stonyfield created the Legacy Program, a series of meetings and exercises designed to immerse employees in the company's mission and culture of teamwork. Events are open to all employees, and all managers are required to attend. Visiting lecturers have included family farmers, the environmental director for outdoor clothing and equipment maker Patagonia, a representative from the National Family Farm Coalition, and financial consultants for socially responsible investing. Through the Legacy Program, employees learn about Stonyfield's mission, discover their own personal connections to it, and determine for themselves how they can move the company closer to its mission in the work that they do.

Stonyfield periodically reviews its internal business practices to make sure that their orientation reflects, and is consistent with, the company's mission. In addition to employing profit sharing, stock options, and open-book finances, the company has even tied employee compensation directly to its mission by instituting a bonus program based on environmental-responsibility goals. As Stonyfield decreases its waste—or increases the percentage of waste that is recycled, employee pay increases; when water and energy use drops per pound of production, employees are granted bonuses.

The Bottom Line

At Stonyfield, it's not enough simply to talk about mission; the company quantifies the extent to which it lives it, constantly measuring its progress toward achieving each of the five elements of its mission, and reporting regularly to its various constituencies. In addition to tracking quality and profitability, Stonyfield has developed a unique set of indicators for consumer education, business education, and employee satisfaction. These including measures such as the number of small family dairy farms the company buys milk from; facility greenhouse gas emissions; percent of organic sales; organic acres supported; employee length of service; and rate of employee turnover.

Stonyfield's success is the story of a company that consistently leads with its mission, and beats the competition in the process. A compelling mission can inspire employees and customers and generate high levels of loyalty from both. According to Gary Hirshberg, "In terms of a branding strategy, as one looks toward the twenty-first century, we can't ignore that consumers are increasingly looking to businesses to solve the world's problems. Companies that are making a true effort to do that are seeing tremendous consumer support."[2] This support is increasingly hitting the bottom line, with increasing customer demand for Stonyfield's products and sustained annual revenue growth rates in excess of 20 percent.

Hirshberg believes that Stonyfield succeeds because employees constantly find ambitious ways to ensure that the company's mission always comes first.

PUTTING THIS PRINCIPLE INTO PRACTICE

Passion inspires an organization's employees to remain motivated in the face of enormous challenges, to stay with a company even when offered more pay or prestige elsewhere, or to accomplish more than employees at more established or better-funded competitors. When employees rally around a company's mission, they tend to go far beyond fulfilling their professional responsibilities by tapping personal reserves of creativity and energy, unleashing a level of performance that can't be achieved in any other way.

There are a number of ways that organizations can foster passionate dedication to their mission. These include giving employees an active role in defining and renewing an organization's mission; taking care to hire people who share a belief in the fundamental purposes and objectives of the organization; encouraging and rewarding 100 percent commitment to the organization's mission; and cultivating a climate of excitement about work. Implementing these approaches, and the five steps that follow, will allow you to tap the vast well of passion that lies within your employees.

Five Steps for Being a Passionate Corporation

STEP 1: Have a mission. If you think your organization is too busy to take on this task, consider hiring help to start the process. When Leonard Pacheco, president and CEO of Bellevue, Washington–based software services consulting firm Excell Data Corporation realized that he needed to develop the company's mission, he hired a consultant who spent thirteen weeks working with all of the company's employees to identify core values (for example, "Don't touch dishonest dollars" and "Treat others with uncompromising truth"). Employee discussion of the outcome led to a shared understanding of the company's true mission: "We solve problems." The consultant was the catalyst the company needed to get the job done. Says Pacheco, whose company grew more than 1,600 percent during the five-year period immediately preceding the mission sessions, "We'd never have found common ground on our own. When your business is exploding, you never have enough time."[3]

STEP 2: Live your mission statement. Most companies today have mission statements, created at no small expense in employee time and company money. Unfortunately, the reality of many businesses, and the actions of the people within them, often differs from the words embossed on these documents. A mission statement should be realistic and attainable, and it should mesh with the values and goals of the organization. According to the Drucker Foundation, a mission statement should be short and sharply focused (in the words of Peter Drucker, an organization's mission should "fit on a T-shirt"); be clear and easily understood; and define why we do what we do and why the organization exists. The foundation cautions against using a mission statement to prescribe means; rather, it should be broad enough to provide direction and address opportunities, while specific enough to focus on competencies. Most important, a mission statement must inspire commitment and define what, in the end, those who adopt it want to be remembered for.[4]

STEP 3: Allow employees to create, review, and renew the mission. Mission statements created by one person at the top often don't work because employees who aren't involved in deciding an organization's direction are usually not personally invested in the outcome. Here are some suggestions for a process that involves all employees in the process of creating, reviewing, and renewing the organization's mission statement:

- Establish a cross-departmental group of employees charged with drafting the mission statement.
- Gather ideas and suggestions for the draft statement from *all* employees.
- Circulate the draft mission statement to all employees and seek their feedback.
- Revise the mission statement to incorporate employee feedback.
- Present the final mission statement to your top management team or board of directors for approval.
- Then, let employees determine how they can best fulfill their mission.

STEP 4: Hire passion. When possible, the easiest way to inject passion into a company is to hire people who already have it. The hiring process provides the best forum for determining if a prospective employee has a passion for your mission. If, like Stonyfield, conditions in your labor market make it more practical for you to develop passionate engagement in your employees after they join your company, look for individuals whose personal interests and skills complement your company's direction.

Step 5: Encourage passion, don't squelch it. A business's mission and values should give employees the opportunity and means to direct their passion for their jobs into activities that benefit their customers and coworkers. At Arlington, Virginia–based AES Corporation, one of the world's leading independent energy producers, shared values rather than formal rules and central control guide individual job performance evaluation, goal-setting, and strategy. AES chose values, including fairness, integrity, social responsibility, and fun that would empower employees, not restrict them. According to business author Bob Waterman, AES's broad values

- have a grab-you-by-the-heart quality that speaks to everyone in the company.
- are evaluated on how effectively they inspire employees.
- continue to evolve as the company grows, changes, and matures.
- enable employees at every level to find creative ways to respond to challenges and lead without specific directives or written policies.
- are consistent with the values most employees aspire to in home and personal life, and help find balance between the needs to feel personal freedom and yet be part of a larger purpose.[5]

Potential Traps and Land Mines

- **Missions imposed on workers from above.** Business owners and top management are responsible for having organizational vision, and they have an inherent right to articulate a mission. But simply having this important organizational piece in place doesn't mean that employees will automatically feel invested—or even connected—to it. In fact, when a company's vision and mission are imposed from above, with no input from those who are expected to work to further them, employees often resist—sometimes strenuously. Vision and mission statements should be progressive in nature—they function best when they undergo periodic discussion and review by *all* members of an organization. When employees are a part of a process that at least seriously considers the possibility of modification, they will feel ownership of the mission and invested in the outcomes. Over time, this inevitably fosters an environment where employees bring greater passion to realizing the organization's goals.

- **Management acting in a way that contradicts the mission.** Employees will quickly withdraw support for an organization's mission when management preaches one way of conducting business, and then acts differently. To encourage employees to embrace the mission, managers need to lead by example and model the mission in their daily business lives. Anything less indicates that the mission is irrelevant, unrealistic, or a badly executed public relations exercise.
- **Raising employee expectations, then deflating them.** Organizations that constantly roll out new management practices and policies in their attempt to increase productivity and teamwork, or to accomplish the latest company priority, risk losing employee engagement. Beyond a certain point, employees become increasingly immune to constant changes in management style, and employee morale can plummet. Unless you're ready to give employees the authority to act on new ideas, be especially cautious of announcing programs and enlisting energetic employees to program teams. Before introducing a new management approach to an organization, first be sure that the change is likely to have lasting impact for your company and industry.
- **Forgetting to have fun at work.** No one will dispute the fact that work is serious business. But humor, fun, and play positively impact workplace productivity, improving morale and retention, and also enhancing customer relations and satisfaction. The Buffalo, New York, office of consulting giant Electronic Data Systems Corporation (EDS) takes fun so seriously that it

recognizes managers who promote a playful work environment with a "Manager of Mirth" award. Criteria for receiving the award include:

1. Creates the culture: Leader appreciates, motivates, and inspires employees.
2. Knows their people: Leader gives creative, timely, and appropriate recognition.
3. Work is fun: Leader finds ways to make serious work—fun!
4. Together we're better: Leader values and fosters creativity and teamwork.
5. Sets the example: Leader has a high sense of self-esteem, is able to take himself or herself lightly, and thereby manages stress more effectively.[6]

Every employee holds some passion for performing well; the challenge is creating a work environment that releases that passion in useful, constructive, and strategically coherent ways. By making employees stakeholders in your company's mission, you'll maximize your company's ability to unlock a unique source of motivation.

10

Coda: Building a Future

Nothing is eternal on the earth below;
And fortune delights in constant change,
So she may more plainly show her power.
—MACHIAVELLI, *CAPITOLO DID FORTUNA*

The organizational structure that Orpheus has evolved to carry out the principles we describe in this book is the result of nearly three decades of research and development, designed to find the most effective ways to fully engage the talents, abilities, and energies of each member of our organization.

Over the years, we have learned a great deal about how to foster creative and effective teamwork. In 1998, we began to explore new links with corporations and academic management programs in the belief that the lessons we have learned could have value for individuals and organizations facing a wide range of business challenges.

We quickly discovered that the principal trends shaping today's business environment are forcing increasing numbers of corporations to confront the very same issues that our organization has dealt with on a daily basis for many years, and our vast experience in knitting together diverse groups of knowledge workers into focused and effective self-managing teams has proven directly relevant to the challenges and concerns that corporations themselves identify as among their most critical, particularly in the technology, media, financial services, and health care sectors.

The Orpheus Process is, among other things, a system that has demonstrated its capacity to sustain dynamic equilibrium between individual freedom and the imperative of cooperation, in a variety of challenging achievement-oriented environments. The results have been excellence in performance, and a high degree of satisfaction among the members of the organization. As self-directed teams have come to play increasingly prominent roles in knowledge organizations of all kinds, the implications of the Orpheus Process's track record of success are far-reaching.

Many employees today have been freed from traditional corporate constraints on innovative thinking, only to face the very different and less familiar challenge of trying to balance individual creative expression with smooth working relationships, to produce harmonious teamwork. For example, the outcomes of corporate mergers often depend on the ability of knowledge workers from profoundly different backgrounds and perspectives to find ways to overcome these differences to work constructively together. This same challenge—finding ways for knowledge workers to overcome differences of training and technical orientation—also confronts corporations that are striving to harness the convergence of disparate technologies to create new products and services.

This, of course, is precisely what we in Orpheus have done for the past three decades, and not surprisingly, corporations that place a high priority on confronting these kinds of challenges have been eager to benefit from the solutions we have developed. By working closely with corporations, we have observed other areas where Orpheus's experience seems particularly relevant. These include:

- Helping individuals to maximize their influence and impact within group process decision-making;
- Helping organizations to enhance their capacity to successfully and efficiently manage complexity by empowering individual workers; and
- Helping corporations to improve retention, morale, and productivity by creating a sense of employee "ownership."

During the past three years, we have observed that even the most hierarchical organizations can benefit from the principles and techniques we have developed—if people are open to change—and we are honored to be considered a model for a new, more effective kind of business organization.

But far from allowing us to rest on our laurels, the process of explaining and codifying our own methodology so it can be understood and assimilated by nonmusicians has forced us to think long and hard about what we do, and what we could do better. Just as corporations have learned lessons from our organization, we too have learned from our interaction with the business world. In addition to provoking us to become more effective communicators and more efficient implementers of our ideas, our unique encounters have fueled a new organizational emphasis on mission-based strategic planning.

We have been especially surprised to discover that individuals working on the cutting edge of today's competitive business environment face challenges that are remarkably similar to those confronting orchestral musicians and other creative artists. To succeed, all knowledge workers require an extraordinary combination of qualities—technical skills that can only be arrived at through years of study, disciplined and precise work habits, and the capacity to let the imagination soar, take risks, and innovate. Focused sharply on our orchestra, we had been accustomed to thinking of these characteristics as unique to our endeavor when, in fact, they are in many respects the defining requirements for successful participation in today's global economy.

The innovators who founded Orpheus boldly set aside two centuries of orchestral tradition and, ever since, experimentation and invention have been essential parts of our nature. Our work with corporations has helped fuel a new era of innovation in Orpheus by bringing us into direct contact with original and effective organizations whose success derives directly from their unconventional and entrepreneurial thinking about new product development, branding, and the marketplace. Their example has inspired us to think creatively and strategically about our place in the world: how we define and serve our markets, utilize new technologies, and reach new audiences.

Orpheus's organizational structure will continue to evolve as we respond to changes in our competitive environment by searching for new ways to meet the needs of our members and our customers. While the ways in which we reinvent the traditional orchestra have already resulted in the many positive changes we have highlighted in this book, the most profound implications for Orpheus lie in the future. The challenge of defining that future continues to excite us tremendously, because it belongs to each one of us.

NOTES

INTRODUCTION: CARNEGIE HALL

1. Ron Lieber, "Leadership Ensemble," *Fast Company*, May 2000, 286.

1: OVERTURE: THE RULES HAVE CHANGED (AGAIN)

1. Peter F. Drucker, "The Coming of the New Organization," *Harvard Business Review*, January–February 1988.
2. Allan Kozinn, "Seeking Harmony in Discord: The Orpheus Ensemble Reconsiders the Way It Makes Music," *New York Times*, 27 October 1999.
3. Frederick W. Taylor, *The Principles of Scientific Management* (New York: Harper Bros., 1911), 5–29.
4. Virginia Postrel, "How Has 'The Organization Man' Aged?" *New York Times*, 17 January 1999.
5. Robert C. Culver, "Empowerment: The Management/Team Interface," Ph.D. dissertation, Claremont Graduate University, Drucker School of Management, 1994.
6. Elizabeth Green, *The Modern Conductor* (Englewood Cliffs, N.J.: Prentice-Hall, 1969), 1.
7. Polly LaBarre, "Leadership—Ben Zander," *Fast Company*, December 1998, 110.
8. Rosamund Zander and Benjamin Zander, *The Art of Possibility* (Cambridge: Harvard Business School Press, 2000), 68.
9. Mark Worrell, "Improvisation in an Anti-Improvisational World," http://www.stringdancer.net/members/guitar/jumpman/improv.shtml.
10. Allan Kozinn, "Seeking Harmony in Discord."

2: PUT POWER IN THE HANDS OF THE PEOPLE DOING THE WORK

1. "To Boost Performance, Turn Employees Loose," *On Achieving Excellence*, November 1991, 10.

2. Allan Kozinn, "Democracy and Anarchy in Concert," *New York Times*, 27 October 1999.
3. John Lubans, "Orpheus Chamber Orchestra," *Duke University Libraries Information Bulletin*, no. 413, 21 November 1997, 6–7.
4. Eli Cohen and Noel Tichy, "How Leaders Develop Leaders," *Training and Development*, 1 May 1997, 58.
5. Charles Gasparino and Jonathan Sapsford, "Hostage to History: As Morgan Persisted in Clinging to Its Past, Time Finally Ran Out," *Wall Street Journal*, 19 October, 2000, A1.
6. Staff, "My Biggest Mistake: Linda Ellerbee," *Inc.*, 1 January 1999.
7. Ed Carberry, "Hypergrowth Strategy: Create an Ownership Culture," *Inc.*, 1 December 1999.
8. John Case, "Corporate Culture," *Inc.*, 1 November 1996.
9. Charles Fishman, "Engines of Democracy," *Fast Company*, October 1999, 174.

3: ENCOURAGE INDIVIDUAL RESPONSIBILITY FOR PRODUCT AND QUALITY

1. Curt Coffman, "Gallup's Discoveries About Great Managers and Great Workplaces," The Workplace Column, *Gallup Management Journal*, 4 February 2000. www.gallup.com/poll/managing/RightPeople.asp.
2. Jan Carlzon, *Moments of Truth* (New York: HarperPerennial, 1987), xv.
3. Ibid., 72.
4. Marcus Buckingham and Curt Coffman, *First Break All the Rules: What the World's Greatest Managers Do Differently* (New York: Simon & Schuster, 2000), 109–11.
5. Dr. Edward Lawler III, "Instilling a Sense of Ownership Among Employees," Foundation for Enterprise Development Conference, October 1991. www.fed.org/resrclib/articles/lawler.html.
6. Beth Fitzgerald, "Taking Ownership Stock Options Are Credited with Increasing Worker Productivity," (Newark, N.J.) *Star-Ledger*, 26 August 1999.
7. Peter Gosselin, "Taking Ownership on the Factory Floor Increasingly, U.S. Workers Are Taking More Risks and Responsibility to Ensure Profits," *Orlando Sentinel*, 30 January 2000.
8. Bob Nelson, *1001 Ways to Energize Employees* (New York: Workman, 1997), 30.
9. David Dorsey, "Change Factory," *Fast Company*, June 2000, 210.
10. Charles Fishman, "Engines of Democracy," *Fast Company*, October 1999, 174.
11. Patrick Kelly, "Forget Policy Manuals," *Inc.*, 1 April 1998.
12. "About Nucor," from the Nucor Web site: http://199.230.26.96/nue/about.html.

4: CREATE CLARITY OF ROLES

1. Laurette Dubé and Leo M. Renaghan, "Surprisingly Simple Routes to the Top," *Cornell Hotels and Restaurants Administration Quarterly*, December 1999, 35.

2. The Ritz-Carlton Hotel Company, LLC, 1999 Application Summary for the Malcolm Baldridge National Quality Award.
3. www.econqa.cba.uc.edu/~evansj/Qnews.htm.
4. Salina Khan, "Ritz-Carlton Opens with Training Tradition, Company President Helps Focus Hotel's Staff on Service," *USA Today*, 29 June 2000, 3B.
5. National Education Association, "Results-Oriented Job Descriptions for Educational Personnel: A New Approach," http://www.nea.org/esp/resource/rojobdes.htm.
6. Bob Nelson, *1001 Ways to Energize Employees* (New York: Workman, 1997, 181–82.

5: SHARE AND ROTATE LEADERSHIP

1. Paul Judy, "Life and Work in Symphony Orchestras: An Interview with J. Richard Hackman," *Harmony*, April 1996, 4.
2. Ibid.
3. Robert Kelley, *The Power of Followership* (New York: Currency Doubleday, 1992), 201.
4. Andrew S. Grove, *High Output Management* (New York: Vintage Books, 1983, 1995), 224.
5. Eli Cohen and Noel Tichy, "How Leaders Develop Leaders," *Training and Development*, 1 May 1997, 58.
6. Michael Kaplan, "You Have No Boss," *Fast Company*, October 1997, 226.
7. Robert Kelley, *The Power of Followership* (New York: Currency Doubleday, 1992), 220.
8. Bob Nelson, *1001 Ways to Take Initiative at Work* (New York: Workman, 1999), viii.
9. Ibid., 155.

6: FOSTER HORIZONTAL TEAMWORK

1. Jon Katzenbach and Douglas Smith, *The Wisdom of Teams* (New York: HarperBusiness, 1993), 9.
2. Peter F. Drucker, "The New Society of Organizations," *Harvard Business Review*, September/October 1992, 95.
3. "Musician Involvement in Symphony Orchestra Organizations," *Harmony*, October 1997, 7.
4. John Lubans, "Orpheus Chamber Orchestra," *Duke University Libraries Information Bulletin*, no. 413, 21 November 1997, 6–7.
5. James A. F. Stoner, R. Edward Freeman, and Daniel R. Gilbert Jr., *Management* (Englewood Cliffs, N.J.: Prentice Hall, 1995), 320.
6. Shari Caudron, "Are Self-Directed Teams Right for Your Company?" *Personnel Journal*, December 1993, 78.
7. Ed Carberry, "Hypergrowth Strategy: Create an Ownership Culture," *Inc.*, 1 December 1999.
8. Bob Nelson, *1001 Ways to Energize Employees* (New York: Workman, 1997), 79–80.
9. Cathy Olofson, "Make Change, Minimize Distractions," *Fast Company*, January 1999.

10. "Values from the Start: Culture Is Strategy at the AES Corporation," excerpted from Bob Waterman, *What America Does Right: Learning from Companies that Put People First* (New York: W. W. Norton, 1994); http://www.aesc.com/print/culture/values/index.html.

7: LEARN TO LISTEN, LEARN TO TALK

1. Deborah Johnson, "Employee Monitoring: Drawing the Line," www.beyondcomputingmag.com/notices/notices2/nethics2.html.
2. www.iwon.com/home/careers/company_profile/0,15623,548,00.html.
3. Intel, "Intel's Culture and Values," http://www.intel.com/pressroom/archive/backgrnd/cn71898c.htm.
4. Kirk Ladendorf, "Intel Inside Austin," *Austin American-Statesman*, 31 March 2000.
5. Anna Muoio, "The Truth Is, the Truth Hurts," *Fast Company*, April 1998, 93.
6. Matt Goldberg, "The Meeting I Never Miss," *Fast Company*, February 1997, 28.
7. Eli Cohen and Noel Tichy, "How Leaders Develop Leaders," *Training & Development*, 1 May 1997, 58.
8. Andrew S. Grove, *High Output Management* (New York: Vintage, 1983, 1995), 71.
9. Paul Roberts, "Getting It Done," *Fast Company*, June 2000, 146.
10. Nancy K. Austin, "The Cultural Evolution," *Inc.*, 15 October 1997.
11. John Case, "Corporate Culture," *Inc.*, 1, November 1996.
12. Anna Muoio, "The Truth Is, the Truth Hurts."
13. Matt Villano, "Shake Up Your Seating Plan," *Fast Company*, October 2000, 60.
14. Scott Kirsner, "Designed for Innovation," *Fast Company*, November 1998, 54.
15. Bob Nelson and Peter Economy, *Managing for Dummies* (New York: IDG Books, 1996), 203.
16. Lewis Eigen and Jonathan Siegel, *The Manager's Book of Quotations* (New York: Amacom, 1989), 39.

8: SEEK CONSENSUS (AND BUILD CREATIVE STRUCTURES THAT FAVOR CONSENSUS)

1. Anna Muoio, "My Greatest Lesson," *Fast Company*, June 1998, 83.
2. GE, "Education at General Electric," http://www.ge.com/news/podium_papers/geleadtrain.htm.
3. Charles Fishman, "Engines of Democracy," *Fast Company*, October 1999, 174.
4. Anna Muoio, "The Art of Smart," *Fast Company*, July–August 1999, 85.

9: DEDICATE PASSIONATELY TO YOUR MISSION

1. Barbara Glanz, *Care Packages for the Workplace* (New York: McGraw-Hill, 1996), 183.
2. Adam Morgan, "The Bigger They Are . . . ," *Success*, February 1999, 64.
3. Nancy K. Austin, "The Cultural Evolution," *Inc.*, 15 October 1997.

4. Drucker Foundation and Jossey-Bass, Inc., *The Drucker Foundation Self-Assessment Tool: Process Guide* (1999), http://www.pfdf.org/leaderbooks/sat/mission.html.
5. "Values From the Start: Culture Is Strategy at the AES Corporation," excerpted from Bob Waterman, *What America Does Right: Learning from Companies that Put People First* (New York: W. W. Norton, 1994), http://www.aesc.com/print/culture/values/index.html.
6. http://www.playfair.com/funatwork.html.

CODA: BUILDING A FUTURE

1. Joe Willke, "The Secrets of New Product Success," *Consumer Insight,* March 1999, http://acnielsen.com/pubs/ci/1999/q1/features/product.htm.

ACKNOWLEDGMENTS

Harvey Seifter and Peter Economy

Leadership Ensemble is first and foremost the story of an exceptional act of collective creation. The credit for inventing the Orpheus Process goes to the members of Orpheus, and each of the hundreds of musicians that have performed with the orchestra over the past three decades has in some way contributed to its ongoing growth and development.

Like every other accomplishment of Orpheus Chamber Orchestra, *Leadership Ensemble* owes a deep debt of gratitude to Julian Fifer and Norma Hurlburt. Julian, along with a group of colleagues, founded Orpheus; without his creative vision and tireless persistence, there would be no Orpheus. For nearly a quarter of a century, that vision was nurtured and sustained by Norma's devoted stewardship as general manager.

The voices of many orchestra members are woven throughout the pages of this book, but the authors are most deeply grateful to Ronnie Bauch, who was a collaborator of profound importance. The historical perspective and finer nuances of musical understanding found herein reflect only two of his enormous contributions to this project.

The evolution of the Orpheus Process from purely musical technique to a model with applicability for the business world has been a remarkable journey, whose success is the result of the efforts of many people. One is Orpheus vice chairman Michael Wiener, whose unique insight into the significance and potential of the Orpheus Process has been an extraordinary resource that we have called upon again and again in recent years. In many ways, Mike's vision was the catalyst behind this book, and he has been unfailingly generous with his time and support throughout its development.

By focusing attention on the broad implications of the Orpheus Process for a wide range of human endeavor, Richard Hackman's pioneering research played a very significant role; Richard also has been very generous with his time and assistance in the development of this book. For the past three years, Orpheus's residency at Baruch College of the City University of New York has functioned as a unique laboratory for exploring the

Orpheus Process as business model, and we are very grateful to Sidney Lirtzman, dean of the Zicklin School of Business, for his encouragement and support.

Orpheus's Board of Trustees provides indispensable leadership to all our activities, and without its generosity and support this book would not have been possible. We are especially grateful to board chairman Gonzalo de Las Heras for his important contributions to the development of this project. We also wish to thank business leaders from several of our corporate partners who have generously shared their unique insights into the Orpheus Process, including John McGeehan (Morgan Stanley), Claus Loewe (J. P. Morgan), Marguerite Copel (Ocean Spray), and Howard Glassroth (ValueOptions).

We would like to thank all the individuals who worked behind the scenes to help line up interviews and coordinate critical schedules at the companies profiled in these pages, including: Silke Mark (J. P. Morgan); Ray O'Rourke, Simon Locke, and Patricia Fawcett (Morgan Stanley); Kate Bryant (Russell Reynolds); Tom Fetter and Peggy Blessing (San Diego Zoo); Vivian Bright (Ritz-Carlton); Jerry Shields and Carol Schumacher (Home Depot); Mary Jo Viederman (Stonyfield Farm); Dennis Slavin (Baruch College); Erin Lehman (Harvard University); Rickie Hall; Stacy Moser-Simpson; and Caran Hardy.

There are others to thank: David Spelman and Scott Waxman for their strategic insight, which gave birth to this project, and their friendship, which helped sustain it through the difficult moments; and our superb and tireless editors, David Sobel and Robin Dennis. We are grateful to all of these individuals for their invaluable contributions. Naturally, any shortcomings in the book are entirely our responsibility.

Harvey Seifter

On a personal note, without the dedicated "above and beyond the call" support of five members of Orpheus's outstanding professional administrative team—Lori Sherman, Valerie Guy, Cynthia Wong, John Wright, and Kendra Miller (who trudged through a snowstorm during Christmas week to type interview notes)—I would never have been able to devote so much of my time to writing *Leadership Ensemble*. I also wish to thank Herbert Weissenstein; in this endeavor, as in so many of my professional activities of the past fifteen years, Herb has been a source of wise counsel and friendship, for which I am most grateful. Above all, my profoundest gratitude is to my wife, Marge, and my daughter, Joanna; without their love and support, I could not have written this book.

Peter Economy

Thanks to my wife, Jan, and my kids, PJ, Sky, and Jack, for their support, and to my mother, Betty, whose own personal story of perseverance is a very real lesson to all who know and love her.

INDEX

INDEX

INDEX

ABOUT THE AUTHORS

Harvey Seifter, a classically trained musician, is executive director of the Orpheus Chamber Orchestra and has successfully managed a number of performing arts organizations in both New York and San Francisco.

Peter Economy is coauthor of *At the Helm: Business Lessons for Navigating Rough Waters* and the best-selling *Managing for Dummies*. He lives in California.

J. Richard Hackman is Cahners-Rabb Professor of Social and Organizational Psychology at Harvard University. With Jutta Allmendinger, Erin Lehman, and Fiona Lee, he has conducted a multiyear study of symphony and chamber orchestras around the world, including the Orpheus Chamber Orchestra.